The Goodness of Affliction

The Goodness of Affliction

Encouragement for Those Who Suffer

David Paul McDowell

Foreword by Margaret Diddams

WIPF & STOCK · Eugene, Oregon

THE GOODNESS OF AFFLICTION
Encouragement for Those Who Suffer

Wipf & Stock
An Imprint of Wipf and Stock Publishers
199 W. 8th Ave., Suite 3
Eugene, OR 97401

www.wipfandstock.com

PAPERBACK ISBN: 978-1-7252-8208-7
HARDCOVER ISBN: 978-1-7252-8209-4
EBOOK ISBN: 978-1-7252-8210-0

Manufactured in the U.S.A.   11/03/20

1 Q. What is your only comfort
in life and in death?

A. That I am not my own,
but belong—
body and soul,
in life and in death—
to my faithful Savior Jesus Christ.

He has fully paid for all my sins with his precious blood,
and has set me free from the tyranny of the devil.
He also watches over me in such a way
that not a hair can fall from my head
without the will of my Father in heaven:
in fact, all things must work together for my salvation.

Because I belong to him,
Christ, by his Holy Spirit,
assures me of eternal life
and makes me wholeheartedly willing and ready
from now on to live for him.

—*THE HEIDELBERG CATECHISM*, QUESTION 1

Contents

Foreword

"IN THIS WORLD NOTHING can be said to be certain, except death and taxes." So goes the pithy quote from a letter penned by Benjamin Franklin back in 1789. However, affliction and its attendant suffering are as universal and as certain as both death and taxes. Indeed, it is the rare adult who has not experienced some form of affliction. A 2014 survey by the American Psychological Association reported that most individuals will be exposed to one or more life-threatening, violent, health, or traumatic events in their lifetime that will upend their well-being and mental health. This appears to be a truth so self-evident that such a survey seems ridiculously unnecessary. But in our day-to-day lives we do not embrace this inevitability. In fact, when afflictions strike, this denial leaves us even less prepared for the havoc that they wreak upon us, our loved ones, and our relationships. When afflictions arise, we don't know how to suffer individually or corporately.

Reading the prophets of old and modern-day theologians, there is no agreement as to why God allows affliction. The purposes for evil are no less important questions even if a definitive answer eludes us. However, given the inevitability and unknown reasons for the existence of affliction, our time is better served when we turn to God to make sense of the suffering it causes. God the Father, in his desire to reconcile the whole world through Jesus Christ, seeks to redeem all, including suffering, for his own good purposes. Paul writes as much in Romans 8:28 to claim God's promise: "And we know that for those who love God all things work together for good, for those who are called according to his purpose." As God is sovereign, there is a purpose for everything in creation. This promise, part of the arc of God's salvific plans, while providing no specific answers, gives us an eternal view and hope, even in the face of suffering. The philosopher Jonathan Lear, in his 2006 book titled *Radical Hope*, notes that such hope is not blind optimism. Instead, he writes that "it is directed toward a future goodness that transcends the current ability to understand what it is. Radical hope anticipates a good for which those who have the hope as yet lack the appropriate concepts with which to understand it." Radical hope is hope without clear understanding. It is practiced through a glass darkly, not known fully, even as we are fully known.

Unfortunately, because affliction strikes in such random ways, our first responses is disbelief. "Why?" and "Why now?" are usually the go-to questions. Without the acceptance of the inevitability of affliction, we want an explanation. God asks us instead to do something akin to radical hope; he wants us to focus instead on finding him in our suffering.

How would our lives differ if we embraced this inevitability of suffering within the greater narrative of God's redemptive purposes? How would our faith be different if we believed deep in our souls that God's love carries us along in our suffering? In its universality, suffering strips us of all our unique identities save that of being children of God. External accolades fall away, well-meaning friends fade into their own fear of inadequacy. As Dave writes, at the heart of suffering is the truth that God alone satisfies.

And while we are at it, what if we actually rejoiced in the face of affliction? Most of us get there, after a while. Once the affliction has passed and the pain, in whatever form it takes, dies down we are able to see markers of growth and resilience: an acceptance of limitations, a greater dependence on God, the ability to take the perspectives of others, even a greater hopefulness and purpose-oriented life. But if we follow the stages of grief, we are more likely to start with denial, and a gut reaction to isolate ourselves from those who can't fathom what we are going through. The isolation is not just from friends and family. We often hide from God at the time when we need him the most and then wonder why he is silent. It's hard to stand before the throne of God when we are not wearing our Sunday best.

Get past the denial and we find ourselves angry at the unfairness of it all. Affliction can have earthly, sin-filled causes. I believe
that we actually prefer when we can identify a cause to others' affliction as it assuages our own fear of its randomness. We want to
believe that a just God would not visit affliction on the righteous,
as if our own sanctification would ward it off, forgetting that he
sends rain on the just and the unjust. Getting past denial and anger, a thin theology that does not stand in awe of God's sovereignty
leads to bargaining with the Almighty, as if we can give God something that he doesn't already offer freely. When denial, anger, and
bargaining fail, we fall into despair. When God is not at the center
of our suffering, this emotional churn is the typical path, increas-
ing the time and distance necessary for us to be able to get to the
place where we can allow God to enter into our grief.

I met Dave early in my career as provost at Wheaton College when he was the chaplain of the graduate school. I knew I
had a friend and confidant from our first meeting. We both had
West Point in common; Dave as the former chaplain, and me as
the mother of a recent graduate. We recognized in each other
the strength and sacrifices that are necessary to support cadets
through their four years at West Point, and later as leaders in our
incomparable army. Dave has the quiet ego strength of someone
who has no need to prove himself to anyone, for he is one who
has emptied himself, taking the form of a servant. The chaplain
for the graduate school is a part-time position. But even though
it was not full-time, it was no less a calling for Dave. He not only
organized the weekly chapel, but his door was open to people like
me, a newbie in an overwhelming role, in a new town with no
friends. I wasn't all that different from the graduate students that
he served. Every time I came into his small windowless office and
sat across from him, I felt safe. God was among us.

Dave was diagnosed with cancer in 2017. It was surreal. Dave,
who exudes energy and optimism, was now tired as chemo zapped
his strength. In this book, he tells us about the exhaustion and fra-
gility to the point that he didn't know how he would stay standing
during his own chapel services. As I witnessed this, it was clear that

Dave was weak, but I never saw a lack of hope or a loss of determination. As we read throughout his book, Dave is not waiting to rejoice as a response to being healed from pancreatic cancer. He is taking Paul's admonition seriously to rejoice in the unknown of the here and now. His journal entries are full of meaning-making in the moment and that is what makes them so honest and powerful. He is praising God because through his suffering, even with forty years of ministry, he has gone to a deeper place of understanding God's love, mercy, sovereignty, and complete sufficiency. Dave wants to share the gifts of his suffering with us. He wants us to experience how much God loves us and has sacrificed for us. He wants us to love Jesus and accept him as our personal savior. He wants us to prepare for the journey that God has called all of us to travel.

That journey is now. Yes, all of us will go through or have gone through times of affliction and suffering that have led to a turning point in our lives. But what if, instead of passively waiting in fear for these precious times of affliction, we sought them out? As the body of Christ, suffering should be corporate; we merely need to follow the prescripts of Christ, invite ourselves into the suffering of others, and our lives will be forever changed, over and over again. We can then rejoice, as Paul wrote to the Corinthians: "We are afflicted in every way, but not crushed; perplexed, but not driven to despair; persecuted, but not forsaken; struck down, but not destroyed; always carrying in the body the death of Jesus, so that the life of Jesus may also be manifested in our bodies" (2 Corinthians 4:9–10).

Dave has invited us to come alongside him in his suffering. He calls us to practice radical hope in the triune God. Thank you for this gift, Dave. It is good to be with you on this journey. You have changed my life.

Margaret Diddams, PhD
Editor, *Christian Scholars' Review*
Principal Consultant, The Diddams Group
September 2020

Preface

A QUICK LOOK AT the get-well card section at CVS culled such messages as "Hope it won't be long at all until the day's at hand, when you're feeling perfect health and really feeling grand." Here is another one: "You ought to get well so you can find, through carefree days ahead, the happiness that you deserve." And then there was a religious message on a very nice card that had a picture on the front of a beautiful country church: "Since God hears every prayer that's said and knows our problems too, then brighter days and better health are just ahead for you."

There is nothing wrong with such messages, apart from some interesting theological implications. I have sent cards like this to sick friends as a gesture of care and encouragement. What happens, however, when your sickness is beyond temporary and your pain goes down deep? All of a sudden these messages convey a completely different meaning. "Is it really possible for me to ever enjoy perfect health again? What does perfect health really mean, anyway? If I am to get well soon, how soon is soon in order to enjoy the happiness I deserve? And if I deserve happiness, why has it been taken away? I know that God answers prayer and knows all my problems; why hasn't he done anything about my situation? Perhaps he doesn't care, or is punishing me, or isn't able to help me."

I am sure that some people might think I am overanalyzing get-well cards. It could very well be, since I have cancer. Suffering, affliction, and terminal disease have a tendency to make you a little sensitive to what well-wishers say. Many become like Job's friends, whose counsel was not so much wrong in theory, but wrong in application.

Ever since my diagnosis with pancreatic cancer in April of 2017, I have wanted to write a brief book on the general topic of suffering in order to encourage those facing dark times the way get-well cards cannot. I wanted to write something deeper, on the level of a booklet written by Thomas Brooks titled *The Mute Christian under the Smarting Rod: Comfort for Suffering Saints*, originally published in 1659. It was not an easy read, because it reminded me of God's sovereignty vis-à-vis my own sin, pride, and the desire to always be in control; and the need for repentance, humility, and submission in the face of my affliction. But it also greatly encouraged me by reminding me of God's kindness and mercy, his constant and covenantal care, and an understanding of affliction as the discipline of a loving Father wanting to shape us more into the image of his beloved Son.

You may have picked up this little book because you are experiencing affliction of some kind. Or you may know someone who is and you think this volume will be helpful. Regardless of why you are reading it, I pray that you will find the same peace and hope that I have found as my journey of discipleship continues and new opportunities to serve others are born out of my own pain.

The chapters in this book are brief and are composed of the blogs I have written over the last several years on my website (davemcdowell.org), having to do directly or indirectly with the subject of suffering. They are not arranged in order, either by topic or by time, but more by flow. It is my prayer that these chapters will be an encouragement to you by helping you see that while God is sovereign and things do not happen "willy-nilly," he is also your Father and nothing can ever separate you from his love.

David McDowell
Lancaster, PA, 2020

Introduction
The Goodness of Affliction

As MUCH AS WE hate to admit it, there is a redeeming factor to suffering. In fact, we could say that in some cases suffering is positively life-changing. A classic example is Alexander Solzhenitsyn, whose writings probably did more to reveal the corruption and emptiness of the Soviet Communist system than any single political factor. He said of his time spent in a Soviet prison camp:

> It was granted to me to carry away from my prison years on my bent back, which nearly broke beneath its load, this essential experience: how a human being becomes evil and good. In the intoxication of youthful successes I had felt myself to be infallible, and I was therefore cruel. In the surfeit of power I was a murderer and an oppressor. In my most evil moments I was convinced that I was doing good, and I was well supplied with systematic arguments. It was only when I lay there on rotting prison straw that I sensed within myself the first stirrings of good. Gradually it was disclosed to me that the line separating good and evil passes not through states, nor between classes, nor between political parties either—but right through every human heart—and through all human hearts . . . That is why I turn back to the years of my imprisonment and say, sometimes to the astonishment of those about me: "Bless you, prison!" I . . . have served enough time there. I nourished my soul there, and I say

without hesitation: "Bless you, prison, for having been in my life!"[1]

"It is good for me that I was afflicted that I might learn your statutes. The law of your mouth is better to me than thousands of gold and silver pieces." (Psalm 119:71–72). "But he knows the way I take; when he has tried me, I will come out as gold . . . I have treasured the words of his mouth more than my portion of food" (Job 23:10, 12).

In these verses we have the experiential testimony of two more sufferers, the psalmist and Job. I have read and pondered these verses for years and am just now coming to understand what they mean.

The goodness of affliction is known (experienced) when God's Word reveals to us who we really are, and becomes more precious to us than all our investments and more necessary to us than our next meal.

One cannot know such goodness without affliction and one cannot benefit from affliction without God's Word. Do not disdain your suffering, but embrace it, for you will nourish your soul there.

"We can ignore even pleasure. But pain insists upon being attended to. God whispers to us in our pleasures, speaks to us in our conscience, but shouts to us in our pain; it is His megaphone to rouse a deaf world . . . No doubt pain as God's megaphone is a terrible instrument; it may lead to final unrepentant rebellion. But it . . . removes the veil; it plants the flag of truth within the fortress of the rebel soul."[2]

May you hear God speak to you in these chapters, as difficult as that might be for you right now. You are not alone on your journey and your suffering is not for nothing.

1. Solzhenitsyn, *Gulag Archipelago*, 615–17.
2. Lewis, *Problem of Pain*, 93.

1

Justice or Wisdom

ONE OF THE REASONS why our suffering can become unusually difficult is because we often look at our situation through the single lens of God's fairness and justice. We are told that righteousness and justice are the very foundation of God's throne (Psalm 89:14), but that is not always evident when we look at our world or at our own difficulties. Perhaps we are not tempted to curse God and die, as Job's wife counseled her husband, but it is hard not to question God's fairness especially when we suffer through no fault of our own. Is it really worth serving him and trying to be an upright person? There seems to be plenty of people in this world who do not love God and yet look like they are healthy and flourishing. Does he really care for me?

In my last read through of the book of Job, a laser beam of truth caught my attention. It wasn't a truth found in the raging argument between Job and his friends, who essentially threw Job under the bus of God's retributive justice. Their singular theme was that people suffer because they have done something wrong and are being punished for it by a God of justice. Their counsel was pretty simple: *Job, fess up and repent, and God will have mercy and restore your health and prosperity* (see Job 11:14; 22:21–23).

Neither was my attention caught by a truth found in the argument of the younger man, Elihu, who also suggested that God was just, but that Job's suffering was remedial. In other words, God uses suffering to wake us up, to save us from walking the wrong path, to correct us, and to lead us to repentance (36:16).

All of these arguments were not wrong in theory, but were wrong in their applicability to Job's situation. Neither these men nor Job were privy to the context of Job's suffering that was introduced to us at the beginning of the book. They did not know what took place in the secret chambers of God's wisdom. Hmmm . . . could it be that we also fail to accurately assess a situation because we do not know what lies beneath or behind it—the wisdom of God?

The truth that caught my attention was found in Job 28, often called the "Great Interlude." The entire chapter is about wisdom (the book of Job is considered wisdom literature) and is the harbinger of God's appearance in chapters 38–41. And guess what? When God does show up, he does not defend his justice but displays his wisdom!

Let us not believe, therefore, that my cancer or your suffering have been allowed by God as a punishment for some sin that we've committed, or else you and I would have died a long time ago. God is not our enemy, but we do have one. In the book of Job he is called the Accuser, and he wants us to curse God and die, or to question the fairness of God, or to impugn his care for us.

We have a choice here, and I choose to trust God for his great wisdom. "Oh, the depths of the riches and wisdom and knowledge of God! How unsearchable his judgments and inscrutable his ways!" (Romans 11:33). Yes, I believe that God is just and fair, but I also believe that his judgments are unsearchable. How can I even begin (like Job and company) to challenge the way God runs the universe or ask why he has allowed something to enter my life that seems to run contrary to his love, mercy, and justice, when I know so little about his ways? In the face of such unfathomable wisdom, I have no place to stand—no footing from which to argue. Instead, I must fall down and worship, like Job eventually did (42:1–6), and submit myself to his unfathomable wisdom.

This is not a pathway of resignation, nor is it merely the passive acceptance of things over which I have no control. Submission to the unfathomable wisdom of God is based upon the reality of my relationship with God through Jesus Christ. My place to stand is holding fast to the covenant he has made with me based upon the life, death, and resurrection of Jesus Christ. I may never know or comprehend all that is happening to me, but I believe that Jesus is my Redeemer and God is my Father. Therefore, I trust that nothing will ever come into my life that has not first passed through his fatherly hand.

Thus, we need to understand our suffering and hardship through the bifocal lens of God's unfathomable wisdom and his great love for us in Christ.

"When Darkness veils his lovely face, I rest in his unchanging grace. In every high and stormy gale, my anchor holds within the veil. His oath, his covenant, his blood, support me in the whelming flood, when all around my soul gives way, he then is all my hope and stay."[1]

1. Mote, "My Hope Is Built" (1834).

2

In a Moment, Life Can Change Forever

A COUPLE OF WEEKS ago I was driving from Annapolis, Maryland, to Strasburg, Pennsylvania—before sunrise. It was a beautiful drive once I got around the Baltimore Beltway into the countryside and onto the serpentine roads of northern Maryland and southern Pennsylvania. As the sun was starting to bulge over the horizon, some of the houses were still mostly dark with just a light or two flickering on as people were getting up for work or school. A new day was dawning. I'm sure that most thought it was just going to be another day of doing the same old thing—at least it was Friday; relief was in sight.

I mused that for some, however, something might take place today that would change life forever. Life would never be the same. Someone might die or receive a diagnosis of a terminal disease. Someone might discover a spousal affair or get divorced. Someone might get fired or go bankrupt; whatever the event, everything would change. Life would be dominated by it—nothing would be able to contend with its significance, not only to an individual but to an entire family. How does one ever prepare for such a thing? How does one cope once it happens?

It brought to mind the lives of two of our next-door neighbors. One was an older lady who had cancer and was one day being picked up by a friend for a chemo treatment. There was no answer when the friend knocked on her door or tried to call on her cellphone. I was in the yard, packing the car for a vacation trip. The friend saw me and asked if I would go into the house and see why the neighbor was not answering her door or phone. I went in, calling her name and heard a muffled "help" coming from the basement. Apparently, our dear neighbor had fallen down the cellar stairs and was lying on the cold cement floor. She was conscious but very weak. She said she had been there since the night before and could not move. I covered her up with more blankets, called 911, and prayed with her until the paramedics came and took her to the hospital. When we returned from our vacation two weeks later, we found out that she had died. Life suddenly changed for her entire family.

A second neighbor, a good man in his late fifties, also fell down his basement steps less than two months ago. His adult sons estimate he had been lying at the bottom of the stairs unconscious for two days before they found him. He never fully regained consciousness. I visited him in the hospital as did some of our neighbors. It was determined that he had injured his brain in the fall and would never regain the use of his limbs. When his organs began shutting down, they brought him home under hospice care. He died last week and we had a very meaningful celebration-of-life gathering for him hosted by his sons. My neighbor and I had talked a few times about eternal things—one time being just after I received my cancer diagnosis. He was open and receptive. I pray that he continued to move toward God. Life has suddenly and radically changed for his family.

I am sure that you can think of more examples of how life suddenly changed for some of your neighbors, friends, and their families—in a moment, in the twinkling of an eye. First there was light ... then came the night. Maybe you have had such an experience.

So, as we turn the lights on every morning wondering if this will be the day life will change, we can do so in one of three ways:

- We can take life for granted and believe that things like this happen to others and not to us—anyway, the weekend is coming.

- We can fear life and what it might bring to the extent that we take no risks, close our hearts to others, and never enjoy the adventure of our journey.

- We can embrace life in all its richness by daily entrusting ourselves into the care of a loving and sovereign God who will not allow anything to come into our lives that has not first passed through his fatherly hand, a God who loves us more than we know and gave himself to us in his Son, Jesus Christ.

In the darkness and uncertainty of Word War II, pastor Helmut Thielicke wrote a small book titled *The Silence of God*. In it there is a sentence that has helped me face my own fear and uncertainty about tomorrow. He said, "If the last hour belongs to God, we do not need to fear the next moment."[1]

1. Thielicke, *Silence of God*, 9.

3

My Feet Had Almost Slipped

HAVE YOU EVER FELT such deep disappointment that led you to believe God was no longer there or had forgotten you? Perhaps it was a situation where you did not particularly like the way God was behaving. Maybe it had not yet come to the surface, but you were simmering inside even though carrying on as if everything was fine. Maybe you are feeling like that right now. You have noticed that your passion for God has started to ebb, you are beginning to lose your desire to be in the Word and pray, you have started to fall asleep in church (much more than usual), and have become critical and hard to live with, and you just do not care much about the things of God.

If you feel this way, Psalm 73 is very important. It is a tale of how a true believer became isolated from God through a crisis of faith. It also shows the process that person (the psalmist) used to restore himself to fellowship.

The psalmist began by *confessing* that God is good. This is important. While he didn't understand the ways of God, he did not stop believing in God. He began with what he knew to be true about God before he proceeded to address the things he did not understand. Many people are not successful with faith-crisis issues because they do not have a firm footing from which to deal with them. Do yourself a favor and don't reinvent the wheel every time you struggle with God. Start your struggle by confessing those things that you know to be true and then proceed from there.

The psalmist then proceeded with his *complaint*. The psalmist was Asaph—writer of twelve psalms and a singer and chief musician in King David's court. Asaph wasn't engaged in a scientific study. He merely looked around and saw the lives of those who did not have a heart for God and it seemed to him that they were getting along just fine, maybe even better than he was. He wondered if it was even worth it to be righteous. He began to get the sense that things just weren't fair and this began to distance him from God.

We do the same thing on a human level. I know some people, for example, who go to church and make the observation that they are the only ones who aren't happy or don't have it all together. Therefore, they feel out of place and stop attending. It is not abnormal to make unsubstantiated assessments about people or situations that cause us to feel a certain way about ourselves. The psalmist did this as he looked around at the health and prosperity of those who did not love God, and it destabilized him. He could not make any forward progress in his relationship to God. Notice how he put it in verse 2: ". . . my feet had almost stumbled and my steps had almost slipped."

A number of years ago, when we lived in New England, I went up on my roof after a snowstorm to shovel off two or three feet of snow along the front edge to prevent an ice buildup. It was melting, so as soon as I shoveled a section it became very slippery. I had to be extremely careful and deliberate with each step because I felt I was about to slip. Finally, it got so bad I could no longer move in any direction; I was completely immobilized. So it is when the feet of faith feel like they are almost slipping—we cannot move in our relationship to God.

And so Asaph poured out his *complaint* before God; he did not broadcast it to others. He realized the effect that such spiritual turmoil could have upon the believing community, especially upon those who were less mature in the faith. Instead, he kept pondering the issue and struggling with it before God until something happened. In verse 17 we read, ". . . I went into the sanctuary of God;

then I discerned their end." We're not told what happened when he went to church that day. We know that he was on the "church" staff, being the chief musician in the temple. Maybe he was leading a worship song that he had sung a million times before, when all of a sudden he gained a new perspective of the Lord. He ceased dealing with God as an object of speculation and began to see him as the subject of worship. He bowed himself before the majestic greatness of God and his whole perspective changed. He bowed and then understood. God was just and the wicked and their wealth would be destroyed.

The psalmist also *confessed* his own humiliation and brokenness: ". . . my soul was embittered, when I was pricked in the heart. I was brutish and ignorant, I was a beast toward you" (vv. 21–22). This is the biblical response when people recognize the presence of God—like Isaiah: "Woe is me for I am lost! For I am a man of unclean lips and I dwell in the midst of a people of unclean lips; for my eyes have seen the KING, the Lord of hosts" (Isaiah 6:5). Or like Peter in Luke 5:8, after he had questioned Jesus' authority and then witnessed his power in the great catch of fish; he fell down before Jesus and cried, "Go away from me for I am a sinful man, O Lord." Or Job's experience: "Therefore I have uttered what I did not understand, things too wonderful for me, that I did not know . . . but now my eyes have seen you; therefore I despise myself and repent in dust and ashes" (Job 42:3, 4).

Similarly, the psalmist *confessed* his humiliation and something else; he also *confessed* the realization that God had always been with him, even though he felt far away (vv. 23–24). God was present with him and would be even in death ("and afterward you will take me to glory"). You can sense the psalmist's growing passion for God in verses 25–26. Asaph turned from the wealth of the wicked that he once envied to his true wealth. "And there is nothing on earth that I desire besides you." God not only satisfies completely, but he remains the true treasure that even death cannot take away.

Do you remember that I told you about being stuck on my roof, feeling that my feet were about to slip? The only way I got out of that predicament was by falling back into the unshoveled snow on my roof. The very thing I tried to get rid of became the very thing I turned to in the end. The psalmist did the same thing with God. He pushed God away and his feet almost slipped. He fell back into God and he found his refuge.

Stay at worship, my friend. Keep in the Word and maintain your prayers, regardless of how you feel, because this is real faith. Hang on to what you know to be true: God is good, he will always be with you, he will never fail you, he is your refuge—he is enough!

4

Elijah vs. Giant Despair

In *Pilgrim's Progress*, the classic allegory of the Christian life by John Bunyan, there is an episode where Christian (the main character) along with his traveling companion, Hopeful, are captured by the Giant Despair, taken back to Doubting Castle (where the giant lived with his wife, Gloom), and thrown into the dungeon. You will need to read that episode for yourself to see the outcome, but I will give you a hint—the Key of Promise. John Bunyan vividly portrayed the discouragement and despair that often overtakes the child of God on the journey to the Celestial City.

In 1 Kings 19, we see the powerful prophet Elijah emotionally and spiritually shriveled by the death threat of Queen Jezebel, after he had singlehandedly defeated 850 of her prophets and priests of Baal in a contest of faith. One would think that Elijah would have been pumped and ready for anything, but his condition revealed the vulnerability and exhaustion that often accompanies great victories in ministry or periods of great demands in life (just as Christian's capture by the Giant Despair followed the trauma of persecution in Vanity Fair and his miraculous escape).

Elijah fled from Jezebel because of fear and went into the wilderness to be alone. The text reveals other symptoms of his condition: he was exhausted, he was ready to quit his job, he was filled with self-pity, and he prayed that he might die. In response, the Lord applied some tender therapy. He touched him, he gave him something to eat, he told him to sleep some more, he touched him again, and gave him more food and drink for the rest of the journey. Compassionate touch, plenty of rest (but not too much), and a nutritional diet was what Elijah's Creator provided for him in this desperate condition. As an aside, I realize that there are those whose depression is more chronic and for whom the afore-mentioned therapy will not help much. I might suggest, however, that compassionate touch may include counseling and the dietary portion may also include the proper use of medication.

Elijah was not out of the dungeon yet. He was still on the run and still alone, although physically he was on the mend. (He was definitely getting lots of exercise.) As he sat in his secure cave on Mt. Horeb, where he knew he would not be found, he was in a bet-ter place to start working through his issues with God. "What are you doing here, Elijah?" God asked. Elijah still engaged in a bit of a pity party about being the only one in all of Israel who remained faithful and was being persecuted. Maybe there was also a hint of complaint that he deserved better from God.

God told him to get out of his cave and stand before him on the mountain. Then he was to listen for God—really, really listen. What great advice when we are discouraged; to get out of our caves, stand before God, and really listen to him instead of our own self-talk. Elijah was able to hear the still and quiet voice of God repeat-ing the same question as before, "Why are you here, Elijah?"

Elijah repeated the very same complaint after hearing God's voice, but somehow it seemed different. Apparently, the Lord saw it was no longer tainted with self-pity, but an honest confession of his condition; a sign that Elijah was ready to be put back in the lineup. So God gave Elijah three ministry assignments: anoint two kings and select a protege. All three tasks had to do with the future; Elijah was out of the dungeon.

There was one more thing that God said, maybe as Elijah was walking away. *Incidentally, you aren't the only faithful one in Israel. There are also seven thousand faithful ones who have not bowed the knee to Baal.* We often need to be reminded that we are not alone either in our suffering or in our faithfulness.

5

How Can I Sing the Lord's Song in a Strange Land?

IN PSALM 137 WE see the sad picture of the Hebrew exiles from Jerusalem, sitting and weeping by the waters of Babylon and being taunted by their Babylonian captors to sing some of their Jewish songs. They responded by hanging up their harps and lyres in the willow trees and asking this question, "How shall we sing the Lord's song in a foreign land?" (v. 4).

It was my third set of CT scans (I got them every three months) after my cancer surgery back in October 2017. While my first scan revealed no cancer, the second one revealed a couple small nodules in my lungs. Therefore, this upcoming scan would show if those little suckers were growing or not. As I sat in the waiting room drinking that horrible barium masked as a fruit drink, I continued to wrestle with my fear and uncertainty. By the way, it does not get any easier to deal with these apart from a fresh exercise of trust and surrender. My prayer was this:

"Once again I surrender myself into your loving care, Heavenly Father, trusting in your plan for my life and in your thoughts for me. Please encourage the faith of others, especially my children, by a good report, and I pray for more years of service in helping to build a future generation of your disciples . . . nevertheless, not my will but yours be done."

I knew that the next day I would be preaching the first message of the academic year to our graduate school chapel community from this passage in Psalm 137. How does one continue in the faith and grow in his or her salvation in the face of difficult situations that make us feel like we are exiles in a strange land? My target audience in chapel was new students, many of whom were internationals, who had been at the school only a week for orientation. They had come to live in this very strange land of academia for the next two to five years depending on their program—far away from home and the familiar, as well as having to learn in the strange tongue of American English. It must have been so difficult for them. But as I sat waiting for my scans, I knew that, no matter the outcome, I would also be preaching to myself living in the strange land of cancer.

I realize how easy it is to "sing my song" in the familiar and while the sun is shining, as Matt Redman suggests in the lyrics to his song: "Blessed be your name when the sun's shining down on me, when the world's all as it should be, blessed be your name." It's far more difficult to sing the second stanza, "Blessed be your name on the road marked with suffering. Though there's pain in the offering, blessed be your name."[1] In fact, how can you sing at all?

And so the next day (Wednesday), I sat in chapel alone as students, staff, and faculty were arriving. I was praying and preparing my heart to preach when I got a text message saying that the nodules in my lungs had not grown and remained unremarkable. Just then, chapel began and soon I was preaching my message with a conviction mixed with relief.

What were the bedrock beliefs that enabled exiles like Joseph, Daniel and his three friends, and Ezekiel to sing the Lord's song in a strange land when no doubt they were also tempted to hang up their harps? I'll give you my main points, but my entire message can be found on YouTube.

- They believed that God was sovereign and that nothing came to them except through his fatherly hand.

1. Redman, "Blessed Be Your Name."

- They believed that God would always keep his covenant promises and would never leave them.

- They believed in prayer and maintained their spiritual practices.

- They believed in the community of fellow sufferers and did not pull away to suffer alone.

I cling to these, especially since those nodules are now growing again. These are weighty matters. Take them to heart no matter in what strange land you find yourself . . . and stay in the community.

6

Beware of Old Clawfoot!

THE TEMPTATION OF JESUS in Matthew 4 is fascinating, especially as we compare it to the temptation of Adam and Eve in Genesis 3. I say Adam *and* Eve because Adam wasn't off playing golf somewhere while Eve was being tempted, but was right there in all of his masculine silence (Genesis 3:6). In Romans 5, Paul actually lays blame for sin entering the world upon the man and not the woman. Thus, you have a sense in the temptation scene in Matthew 4 that Jesus is the "Second Adam"; he is God's Champion fighting to win back the territory lost to Satan by the first Adam.

What is striking is the contrast between the two temptation scenes. Genesis 3 occurs in the midst of a garden of plenty, the only place in human history where the phrase "It doesn't get any better than this" would have been an accurate description. The two humans were fat, full, and free. Jesus, on the other hand, was in a desert wilderness, not a garden; he was alone and hungry after fasting for forty days. This contrast shows us that Old Clawfoot (I'm not talking about bathtubs) can come at us whether we are in plenty or in want, happy or suffering, married or single.

Where the two scenes converge is with the temptation itself. In both cases, Satan attacks the goodness and trustworthiness of God. To Adam and Eve: "Did God actually say, 'You shall not eat of any tree in the garden?'" (Genesis 3:1). Satan implied, "What kind of God would put you in a beautiful place of abundance and then tell you that you can't have what you see? Go ahead and help yourselves to what you desire; it won't hurt you. In fact, it will be empowering and fulfilling; it's not wrong; it will give dignity and equality." To Jesus: "If you are the Son of God, command these stones to become loaves of bread" (Matthew 4:3). Satan implied, "Didn't God just tell you that you were his beloved Son? And now look at you: alone, hungry, and desolate. Is that any way to treat your son? What kind of Father is he? Take things into your own hands and make these stones into bread. You have the power."

In both cases Old Clawfoot sought to insinuate that God didn't care for his sons and daughter by calling into question the Word of God. Satan did the same thing in the book of Job, where he questioned the Word that God spoke about his servant Job by insinuating that the only reason why Job was faithful was because he knew where his bread was buttered. In other words, God is not worthy to be worshiped for who he is unless he pays off his worshipers with benefits. Satan said, "But stretch out your hand and touch all that he has, and he will curse you to your face" (Job 1:11). He said essentially the same thing in Job 2:5.

One thing you can always bank on is that Satan hates God and is jealous of God's position. His deepest desire is to be worshiped and this was made abundantly clear in the third temptation of Jesus. Thus, while Satan's strategy changes from person to person and situation to situation, what remains the same are his lies and insinuations about God and his goodness. He will always tempt us to doubt God's Word and to act independently of God's provision. Remember that Satan is a liar (the father of lies) and will offer you anything because he never has to make good on those promises. He is incapable of speaking the truth; truth gets stuck in his throat. He may promise you the moon but in the end you will have nothing but moldy cheese.

So, are you in a good place in your life right now? Beware lest you be tempted to believe that you have gained "great and good cities that you did not build . . . cisterns you did not dig, and vineyards and olive trees you did not plant—and when you eat and are full, take care lest you do forget the Lord" (Deuteronomy 6:11–12). Instead, give him thanks and do not cease in your worship and praise for his goodness and provision. "We give thee but thine own, what 'er the gift may be; all that we have is thine alone, a trust, O Lord, from Thee."[1]

In contrast, perhaps you are in a place of pain or suffering some kind of deprivation; beware lest you are tempted to believe that God does not care what you are facing or that you are being punished for your sins so that you are on your own to find relief. I am reminded of how Solomon Northrup (*Twelve Years a Slave*) hung on to his identity as a beloved son of God in spite of the horrors of his being kidnapped and enslaved during the Civil War.

We must never forget that the way of the cross is often a way of pain, because our discipleship calls us to submit to the lordship of Jesus rather than succumb to the pressures of prevailing culture, which has been usurped by the god of this world.

> Adopted as children of God and called to follow in the way of the cross, we are all summoned to various forms of self-denial. The struggle against disordered desires, or the misdirection of innocent desires, is part of every Christian's life . . . Often these are not open to choice, but are given us as a situation in which we are to live faithfully. We are not promised that the struggle will be quickly and triumphantly resolved . . . only that it will be crowned at last by a character formed through patience like Christ's.[2]

Let us not lapse into self-pity or listen to the plausible arguments of Old Clawfoot. Let us instead, like our Savior, listen to the Word of God: "Fear not little flock, for it is your Father's good pleasure to give you the kingdom" (Luke 12:32). "Let not your hearts be troubled. Believe in God; believe also in me [Jesus]" (John 14:1). Nothing "will be able to separate us from the love of God that is in Christ Jesus our Lord" (Romans 8:39).

1. Howe, "We Give Thee but Thine Own" (1858).
2. Church of England Evangelical Council, "St. Andrews Day Statement."

7

The Sound of My Groanings

"Because of my loud groaning, my bones cling to my flesh. I am like a desert owl of the wilderness, like an owl of the waste places, I lie awake; I am like a solitary sparrow on a housetop" (Psalm 102:5–7). There is a sleep-related condition called *catathrenia* in which a person makes a groaning sound that can last up to forty seconds in one exhale, ending in a sigh or a grunt. It is not related to snoring (an inhale issue) and it doesn't interrupt sleep, except for the person with whom the groaner is sleeping.

The psalmist, however, depicts a circumstance in which his groans were the result of deep suffering and affliction accompanied by an inability to eat or sleep. In addition, he felt isolated and alone, much like an owl whose very appearance seems downcast and which seeks habitats of desolation. While we do not know the situation that generated the writing of this psalm, verses 18–20 may provide a hint "that God looked down from His holy height . . . to hear the groans of the prisoners, to set free those who were doomed to die."

Perhaps the writer had a Dostoyevsky-like experience where he was rescued at the last moment from a firing squad. Whatever the circumstance, the beauty of his lament is in its focus on the eternity and faithfulness of God. Though the earth and the heavens will wear out like an old garment, God will remain the same, "and your years have no end" (v. 27). This has led someone to say that we can only truly praise God when we can trust him with our lament.

When was the last time you groaned before God? Perhaps it was when you were facing bitter disappointment, enduring chronic or acute pain, or enduring personal struggle or tragedy. Such situations tend to isolate us and make us feel like barn owls while everyone around us seems to be happy, healthy, and successful. Such a situation forms the basis for the psalms of lament. Such psalms reduce our sense of isolation because they put us in communication with multitudes of others who have suffered. The psalms of lament also give us a framework so that our sadness does not become a barrier but a bridge to God, who loves us, yet also allows evil to exist so that he can use it for his good purposes.

Let me suggest that you investigate some of the psalms of lament: 4, 10, 12, 13, 44, 60, 74, 79, 80, 83, 85, 90, 102, 123, 126, 129. Pray through one of these out loud and use it as the sound of your own groaning. When you do this, you will realize that you are not alone in your lament; you will join a vast host of saints throughout the ages using this very psalm. It will also be an opportunity for you to affirm the character of God that you see revealed therein and revel in his love for you in Christ.

Through your groaning, the Holy Spirit will also articulate your deepest needs to the Lord Jesus Christ, who will intercede for you before the Father (Romans 8:26, 34). "Weeping may tarry for the night, but joy comes with the morning" (Psalm 30:5).

8

Disappointment with God

Then Moses turned to the Lord and said, "O Lord, why have you done evil to this people? Why did you ever send me? For since I came to Pharaoh to speak in your name, he [Pharaoh] has done evil to this people, and you have not delivered your people at all" (Exodus 5:22–23).

CAN YOU FEEL MOSES' disappointment and frustration? Do you remember a time when you felt like this—maybe even now? Perhaps it was a situation about which you earnestly prayed and things got worse. I think that Christian leaders often fall prey to this disappointment when all our best-intentioned efforts and ministry to our people end up being misunderstood and creating more problems than they solve. We make the mistake, like Moses, of judging God at the beginning of the process and not by the big-picture vision of what he ultimately wants to accomplish in our people. We have so little information as to the ways of an eternal, omniscient God. Perhaps that is why Moses later prayed, "Show me now your ways" (Exodus 33:13).

Another principle that we need to learn is that the way to liberation is often through deeper bondage. That sounds strange, doesn't it? However, how many times have we heard (or experienced) that a person needs to hit bottom before they start looking for help? Israel had not yet hit rock bottom in their slavery. They thought they had options and had to learn to entrust themselves completely to the covenant-keeping God whom Moses represented. Moses also needed to learn to trust in the Lord with all his heart if he was going to lead Israel out of oppression. "God is to be trusted when his providences seem to run contrary to his promises."[1]

We cannot manage God; we must learn to trust him. He is our Father, who loves us and yet is also the sovereign God of the universe working out his redemptive process for us and for the world. It is only by faith born of experience that we will learn to glory in the process and not judge God by a certain circumstance.

"You fearful saints, fresh courage take; the clouds you so much dread are big with mercy and shall break in blessings on your head. Blind unbelief is sure to err and scan his work in vain: God is his own interpreter, and he will make it plain."[2]

1. Watson, *Body of Divinity*, 120.
2. Cowper, "God Moves in a Mysterious Way" (1773).

9

Wasted Pain

CHARLOTTE ELLIOT LIVED AT the close of the eighteenth century and in great physical pain most of her life because of a childhood illness. She also struggled with bouts of depression. An old family friend once asked her whether she had ever come to know the peace of God through faith in Jesus Christ. She became defensive, upset that anyone would dare ask such a question, but after cooling down she admitted her need of spiritual help. She confessed her desire to receive Christ and said, "I want to come to Jesus, but I don't know how." Her friend replied, "Come to him just as you are." She did and experienced the peace of God in her life in spite of her many struggles.

One Sunday she was at home, unable to attend church because of her pain. She took a pen and paper and began to write these words: "Just as I am, without one plea, but that Thy blood was shed for me. And that Thou bidd'st me come to Thee, O Lamb of God, I come! I come!" She published this hymn anonymously in a small Christian newspaper, and it began to gain popularity all over England.

One day her doctor handed her this poem, thinking it would be of encouragement, and she recognized it as her own. She began writing more hymns of encouragement and invitation. Her pain became the source of a deeper walk with God and a wellspring of opportunity for ministry to others. A century later a young man named Billy Graham went forward to receive Christ when this hymn was sung.

Is your pain being wasted? How could God use it for his glory and the eternal good of others?

10

God of the Stars,
God of the Brokenhearted

THE INCARNATION TEACHES US that God became flesh and dwelt among us. The infinite, eternal God became one of us and fully entered into our human situation so that he might redeem us. I think we still have this mythological notion that if we are facing difficulties, feeling depressed and experiencing life's unfairness, then our Christmas will be ruined. I'm going to make a bold statement: it isn't until we do experience these things that we will understand the true nature of the incarnation; that the God of the stars has become the God of the brokenhearted.

The birth of Christ was revealed to the outcast, the old, the brokenhearted, and the dispossessed. This is the truth of the Christmas story: God stooped so low in Jesus that no one is excluded from his grasp.

I want to take you back to Christmas Eve 1944. The place is the Dachau concentration camp, where a German Lutheran pastor, Martin Niemöller, has been held prisoner for seven years because of his involvement in the Confessing Church. Niemöller was the man who wrote the now-famous lines, "First they came for the Socialists, and I did not speak out, because I was not a Socialist. Then they came for the Trade Unionists, and I did not speak out, because I was not a Trade Unionist. Then they came for the Jews and I did not speak out, because I was not a Jew. Then they came for me, and there was no one left to speak for me."[1]

Listen as Pastor Niemöller preaches to his congregation of skeleton-like figures huddled around him in their cold, dark bunkroom on a less-than-perfect Christmas Eve:

> God, the eternally wealthy and almighty God, enters into the most extreme human poverty imaginable. No man is so weak and helpless that God does not come to him in Jesus Christ, right in the midst of our human need; no man is so forsaken and homeless in this world that God does not seek him, in the midst of our human distress . . . This is what is so singularly peculiar in the Christian message of salvation, which tells us, "You need not go to search for God; you should not imagine that he is far from you and is not concerned with what crushes you! He is here and is close to you in the man who, as a babe wrapped in swaddling clothes, was lying in a manger. All your need is so far from being alien to him that, on the contrary, he gave himself freely to bear it with you." Whoever can grasp this in faith is not forsaken in prison and in death; for in the worst darkness he may say, "Thou art with me; thy rod and staff they comfort me."[2]

It is the people who walk in darkness who will see a great light. It the people who live in a land of deep darkness who will have a light shine upon them (paraphrase of Isaiah 9:2). O blessed incarnation!

---

1. Niemöller, "First They Came . . ."
2. Niemöller, "Dachau Sermon Christmas Eve," 55–56.

11

Pleasing God in Our Suffering

ALL CHILDREN WANT TO know if they please their parents. This is certainly true of young children, whose very identity is shaped by the affirmation and attention of a mom and dad, but I also believe this is true of us even as we get older. I remember the time when I was in my thirties and I had spoken in chapel at Wheaton College, Illinois. My mom had sent for the tape of my message and when she received it she called me with delight. Billy Graham had spoken the week before and so his message was on the tape as well. Mom said, "David, you'll never guess who they put on the backside of your tape!" Well, I knew who was on whose backside, but my mom affirmed me as only a mother could.

In the same way, I believe that every child of God desires to know whether they please their Heavenly Father. We go to great lengths to evaluate our actions and measure our behavior. The problem is that we tend to do this evaluation by our standards, which are tinged with self-focused guilt and cheap-grace legalism. The times I think I am most pleasing to God may be the times I am most lifted up with pharisaical pride. The times when I feel I am the most despicable me may be the very times when I please him the most. This makes John's counsel wise indeed: "for whenever our hearts condemn us God is greater than our hearts, and he knows everything" (1 John 3:20).

And so I go round and round, like a gerbil on its wheel. Is there any recourse, any truth that would help me stop wasting time in taking my spiritual pulse and finding a false heart rate? Yes. The truth is found in two prepositional phrases that characterize Paul's understanding of Christianity: *in Christ* and *Christ in me*. I want to focus on what it means to be "in Christ" and how it relates to pleasing God. The person in Christ is the one who believes in the gospel and through that faith has entered into a union with Christ in his death, burial, and resurrection. "God made him who had no sin to be sin for us, so that in him we might become the righteousness of God" (2 Corinthians 5:21).

When a person comes to see him/herself as a sinner and believes that Jesus Christ's death, burial, and resurrection has dealt once and for all with his/her sin and guilt, there is a divine relational transaction that occurs. The believing sinner comes into a faith union with God's Son so that *all we are in our sinful humanity* becomes swallowed up in *all that Christ is* in his righteous relationship with the Father.

Victor Raymond Edman tells the story of the banker whose son was a soldier in the Union Army during the Civil War. One day another soldier walked into the bank and up to the father's desk and handed him a note. The young soldier was dressed in a tattered uniform and his arm was in a sling from a wound. The note read: "Father, this is my friend who is like a brother to me. He was wounded in our last action. Please take care of him; treat him as you would me. Love, Charlie." The father recognized the handwriting of his son and took the young soldier and put him in Charlie's room to rest, gave him Charlie's clothes for dress, and seated him in Charlie's place at the table to eat. This young man was beloved for the sake of Charlie.[1] Likewise, we are loved for the sake of Christ.

I have often used an illustration of taking an ink-splotched piece of paper, representing my sinful self, and placing it into my open Bible, representing Christ and his righteousness. The act of faith is depicted as putting the paper into the book and closing it.

1. Blanchard, *Getting Things from God*, 101–2.

Thus, when God looks at me, whom does he see? Christ. Whatever relationship Christ has with the Father, I have with the Father. Christ's history becomes my history; his future is my future. By faith, the very righteousness of Christ becomes my righteousness. "But now a righteousness from God, apart from the law, has been made known, to which the Law and the Prophets testify. This righteousness from God comes through faith in Jesus Christ to all who believe" (Romans 3:21–22).

Paul uses the legal term "justify" for describing what happens when we believe the gospel. He never infers that righteousness is somehow *infused* into us when we believe in Christ so that we actually become righteous. The Bible teaches that through faith God *imputes* or places the righteousness of Jesus Christ on our account and we become "just-as-if-I'd" never sinned in relationship to God. And herein was Martin Luther's certainty and mine as well. If my salvation comes as the result of what Christ has done for me, then I have the complete assurance of knowing that it is enough. The more my relationship to God depends upon my efforts, the less certainty I have of my acceptance with God. Have I done enough? Am I sorry enough? That is why we see the cry of Martin Luther to the recovered gospel: *Sola gratia, sola fide, solo Christo.*

Thus, the first thing we need to do when taking our spiritual pulse is not to ask whether God loves and is pleased with me, but whether God loves and is pleased with Christ. And since we know the answer to that question and I am in Christ, therefore I may have the confidence of knowing that God loves me today and will always be pleased with me as his daughter or son in Christ! It is by this standard of measurement that "the Spirit himself bears witness with our spirit that we are the children of God, and if children, then heirs—heirs of God and joint-heirs with Christ, provided we suffer with him in order that we may also be glorified with him" (Romans 8:16–17). Did you notice the last part of this verse, ". . . provided we suffer with him"? Sometimes we doubt God's love for us because we suffer, but here we are assured that our family crest includes suffering as well as glory.

12

Why I Hope to Die at Seventy-Five

Ezekiel "Zeke" Emanuel recently wrote an interesting article in *The Atlantic* headlined "Why I Hope to Die at 75." It is worth the read, especially if you are approaching seventy-five or have parents or grandparents that age. Emanuel is a doctor, bioethicist, and older brother of the former mayor of Chicago, Rahm Emanuel.

His basic premise is that by seventy-five creativity, originality, and productivity are pretty much gone. We no longer leave behind a legacy of vibrancy and engagement, but of feebleness and instability. Not only do we load our children down with additional emotional and financial burdens, but we leave them and our grandkids to remember us by our frailty, which he calls "the ultimate tragedy." Therefore, he does not wish to live beyond seventy-five.

He does not advocate for euthanasia, but it is his plan (he is now seventy-five) that if he lives to seventy-five he will not prolong his life.

> At 75 and beyond, I will need a good reason to even visit the doctor and take any medical test or treatment, no matter how routine and painless. And that good reason is not "It will prolong your life." I will stop getting any regular preventive tests, screenings, or interventions. I will accept only palliative—not curative—treatments if I am suffering pain or other disability . . . This means

colonoscopies and other cancer-screening tests are out
. . . If I were diagnosed with cancer now, at 57, I would
probably be treated, unless the prognosis was very poor.
But 65 will be my last colonoscopy. No screening for
prostate cancer at any age . . . After 75, if I develop cancer,
I will refuse treatment; similarly, no cardiac stress test.
No pacemaker and certainly no implantable defibrillator.
No heart-valve replacement or bypass surgery. If I develop emphysema or some similar disease that involves
frequent exacerbations that would, normally, land me
in the hospital, I will accept treatment to ameliorate the
discomfort caused by the feeling of suffocation, but will
refuse to be hauled off . . . Flu shots are out . . . no to
antibiotics. Obviously, a do-not-resuscitate order and
a complete advance directive indicating no ventilators,
dialysis, surgery, antibiotics, or any other medication—
nothing except palliative care even if I am conscious
but not mentally competent—have been written and
recorded. In short, no life-sustaining interventions. I will
die when whatever comes first takes me.[1]

While I agree with him about the American obsession with
living forever, he falls off the other side of the saddle with his
American obsession with control. He sees the eighteen years that
he has left (as if he is in charge) as a self-imposed deadline, so that
he can get done the important things in life before he begins his
inevitable decline. He is also dismissive of any faith perspective
that would be used to rebut his view.

"I also think my view conjures up spiritual and existential
reasons for people to scorn and reject it. Many of us have sup-
pressed, actively or passively, thinking about God, heaven and hell,
and whether we return to the worms. We are agnostics or athe-
ists, or just don't think about whether there is a God and why she
should care at all about mere mortals."[2]

He seems to make a life of faith seem more like a knee-jerk
reaction to our mortality rather than well-intentioned choice in

1. Emanuel, "Why I Hope to Die at 75."
2. Emanuel, "Why I Hope to Die at 75."

view of our creatureliness and frailty. He also completely overlooks the positive impact that our suffering can have in the development of our children, grandchildren, and others who watch to see how we live and how we die.

There is an arrogance embedded in this article that belies the name of the author, Ezekiel (which means his strength is in God). The prophet Ezekiel was keenly aware of God's presence and power in human affairs. He suffered captivity and the very death of his own wife, but prophesied a message of hope and reassurance for the people of Judah. There was one thing that the biblical Ezekiel knew for sure: God is in control and we must humble ourselves before him. And in this relationship of submission, humility, and trust regardless of life's circumstances, we find our greatest usefulness.

"So teach us to number my days that we may get a heart of wisdom" (Psalm 90:12)

13

O for a Heart That Craves God!

THE PSALMS REFLECT THE wonder of life, the glory of creation, the incomparable gifts of God, praise for his love and constant care. But they also reflect the loneliness of the human spirit, which no earthly medicine can heal; the solitude of mental anguish; the hours of dark despair; the waves of doubts and fears upon which all men and women are tossed.

In the preface to his *Commentary on the Psalms*, John Calvin wrote in 1563: "I may truly call this book an anatomy of all parts of the soul, for no one can feel a movement of the spirit that is not reflected in this mirror. All the sorrows, troubles, fears, doubt, hopes, pains, perplexities, stormy outbreaks by which the hearts of men are tossed, have been depicted here."[1]

As we have already seen, the psalms that most closely fit this description are called psalms of lament. These psalms mirror the painful emotions of the soul struggling with circumstances beyond its control and trying to reconcile such situations with what it believes about God.

Lament psalms are of two kinds. The first kind express the lament of the nation as a whole, for example, Psalm 44: "Awake! Why are you sleeping, O Lord . . . Why do you hide your face? Why do

---

1. Calvin, *Commentary on the Psalms*, xxxvi–xxxvii.

you forget our affliction and oppression?" Then there are the individual or personal lament psalms, which follow a typical pattern:

- An introduction—usually a cry for help
- A lament—a description of the complaint
- A remembrance of what is known to be true about God
- A petition—asking God for something
- A confession of trust

Such a pattern should be a model for our own communication with God in the midst of discouragement or despair. These psalms should teach us that we can bring such things before God, indeed, that we must come before God at times like this. They will help us to work out our anger and despair within the context of our faith rather than outside of it.

An example of such lament is Psalms 42 and 43, which were (most likely) one psalm with three *strophes*, each with twelve lines concluding with an identical refrain: "Why are you cast down O my soul, and why are you in turmoil within me? Hope in God; for I shall again praise him, my salvation and my God."

The psalmist feels that he is separated from God (from the temple in Jerusalem). He feels this so intensely that he describes it in physical terms—like a thirsty deer trying to find water in a dry and arid land. The psalmist is both spiritually and emotionally thirsty for the presence of the living God. In verse 3, his grief finds expression in his tears; in fact, his condition is such that he has been doing more weeping than eating ("my tears have been my food day and night"). Have you ever thirsted for God? Even if you don't think so, I believe that you have but were just not aware of it. I believe that a desire to be personally related to God is a basic human drive and the reason why we have been created.

The problem is that this thirst for God is masked behind other human desires. I can prove this by showing that the fulfillment of every human desire does not lead to permanent satisfaction. In fact, our human cravings may actually cause us to hate the very thing we thought we loved. Let's do a little experiment. Let's say you have a craving for mint chocolate-chip ice cream. "I'd do anything for some," you say. And I reply, "OK, here are five gallons and one spoon, and you must eat it all." Let's say for argument's sake that you do—you eat every bit of the ice cream, then gag. How do you think you would be feeling about your desire for mint chocolate-chip ice cream? Satisfied? You probably wouldn't use that word to describe your feeling. You would most likely say, with great emotion, "I never want to see or smell another spoonful of ice cream again!"

There is a story in 2 Samuel 13 about a man named Amnon (one of King David's sons), who was "in love" with his half-sister Tamar. He told one of his friends, "I love Tamar, my brother Absalom's sister" (v. 4). He loved her so much that he couldn't eat. So he went to bed pretending to be sick and asked that Tamar be sent to feed him. She came into his bedroom and he forced sex upon her. "Then Amnon hated her with a very great hatred, so that the hatred with which he hated her was greater than the love with which he had loved her" (v. 15). And then he told her to get out of his presence and he locked the door of his room. That was love?

The analogy of the ice cream and the tragic story about Tamar illustrate the same point: human desire cannot be ultimately satisfied by the thing it craves, because we were not made for ice cream, or sex, or drugs, or money and fame, but for God. C. S. Lewis said it so well in his *The Problem of Pain*: "If I find in myself a desire which nothing in this world can satisfy, I must conclude that I was made for another world."[2] Behind every human desire there is a thirst for God.

God said to Israel, "Come, everyone who thirsts, come to the waters . . ." (Isaiah 55:1). Jesus said, "If anyone thirsts, let him come to me and drink" (John 7:27).

---

2. Lewis, *Problem of Pain*, 135.

14

Death Be Not Proud

A NUMBER OF YEARS ago, my wife and I (and our daughter and granddaughter) had the privilege of attending the memorial service for Pastor Jerry at College Church, Northampton, Massachusetts. Jerry and I were associates in ministry there for twelve years, along with another associate, Tim. Jerry's life was a tribute to God's amazing grace and his influence was deeply profound.

Jerry came to Christ one Easter Sunday at College Church. He responded to the gospel and God saved him out of a life of alcohol and drugs. He was given a thirst for God that could not be quenched. He began working as the janitor at College Church. He attended Berkshire Christian College in Lenox, Massachusetts, and realized his calling to pastoral ministry. We asked him to serve as our assistant minister and then he became my associate, serving alongside Tim. The three of us were together in ministry for over a decade in the 1980s and 90s and made a great team. We did not always see eye to eye, but we always stood shoulder to shoulder in our respect for one another and our love for our people. Those were days of challenge and growth, and we saw much fruit in our labor together in the unique environment of Northampton—a place that birthed the Great Awakening and heard the preaching of Solomon Stoddard, Jonathan Edwards, and George Whitefield, and yet had become the polar opposite of this wonderful heritage.

Jerry grew as a pastor, preacher, and theologian who loved the doctrine of God's sovereign grace. He was awed by a holy God. While overwhelmed by his own sinfulness, Jerry was also filled with joy at the love and mercy of God. He was ever desirous of living a holy and useful life. He married, and he and Mary Ellen began their journey as a very effective ministry team that continued right up until Jerry went to be with Jesus. However, their ministry was attended by much suffering, especially because of Jerry's health issues—the kind of suffering that few of us have ever experienced.

Soon after they were married, Jerry had to go on dialysis because of kidney failure. There were days he came to work with eyes so bloodshot that it made your own eyes water just to look at them. Yet he never complained about the "hand he had been dealt." He believed that God was sovereign and that his suffering was designed to purify and perfect, not to punish. Jerry's attitude embodied the psalmist's in Psalm 119:71: "It is good for me that I was afflicted, that I might learn your statutes."

God graciously provided a new kidney and proceeded to bless them with four very special children: Rachel, Grace, Molly, and then Ben. They loved their dad and knew that he loved them. He worked hard as a pastor, and even moonlighted to supplement his salary so that his kids could go to the Jonathan Edwards Academy, which Jerry and Mary Ellen helped to found. He also became and remained the pastor of our second daughter church, Christ Church, located in Greenfield, Massachusetts.

The specter of infirmity did not leave him for long. Mary Ellen struggled with her own health as kidney issues continued for Jerry. Then there was cancer, surgeries, treatments, and more cancer. His wonderful church loved and supported him and his family, and Jerry kept preaching; his sermons ever deepening because more of God's majesty was being revealed in his own infirmity. When you sat with him the conversation wasn't focused on his issues, but on you and how you were doing. Besides his hope of eternity, he hoped that he would live long enough to see the birth of his grandson. His hope was fulfilled just before he died. He even got to hold his little Elijah.

In the end, he struggled with death, which took his family by surprise. Perhaps we expect a godly man who loves Jesus to pass from this world peacefully—and some do. However, we need to remember that death is still the enemy and we are all a bunch of amateurs. Our experience will be unique to us as will the circumstances of our infirmity. In John Bunyan's *Pilgrim's Progress*, Christian had a completely different kind of experience than his friend Hopeful as they crossed the River of Death. Christian was filled with terror, while Hopeful felt the bottom of the river right away and was able to walk across. Hopeful called out to Christian to take courage and not to fear. "Brother, I feel the bottom, and it is good!"

Jerry was not a flash-in-the-pan man, but a faithful and solid man. He was only a year younger than me, and so his death is a vivid reminder that I will soon follow him across that river. Such a thought does not disturb me, in part because I saw how Jerry faced his suffering.

15

The Greater Jihad

WHEN WE HEAR THE word *jihad* our minds race to the horrific scenes of 9/11 or to the many other acts of terror that have been perpetrated in the name of religion. However, some Muslim scholars have distinguished between the "lesser jihad," which is the struggle against the enemies of Islam, and the "greater jihad," which is the inner personal struggle against sin and to fulfill one's religious duties. I have spoken with my some of my Muslim friends who believe that it is this internal suffering as one struggles with human nature which is the true understanding of jihad (*al-jihad fi subil Allah*; striving in the way of God).

There is a certain affinity here with our Christian understanding of sanctification, which is the divine process or work in the soul of the believer whereby he/she comes to exhibit the life and character of Jesus Christ. Sanctification is composed of two basic realities that are at play within us at the same time: mortification and quickening. Mortification is where we cooperate with the Holy Spirit in "crucifying the old man." "Putting to death the flesh" and "denying ourselves" are other ways of describing the ongoing struggle against our sinful human nature. At the same time, God's Spirit continues to quicken our souls with new life, where our desire for holiness increases and where a new course in life is set and promoted. Someone has likened it to the old structures of sin being torn down and the new structures of God gradually erected. Sanctification is a work of God, but we are engaged in the process—and it is a struggle.

I think we have failed to realize what a struggle it is to be a follower of Christ. We tend to define suffering in the Christian life as the result of persecution or the effects of sin and sickness in this world. Rarely do we hear of struggle and suffering as part of the drama of discipleship as we say "no" to our nature's attachment to this world and "yes" to the narrow gate obedience to God (Luke 13:24). In fact, we are almost embarrassed to talk of our struggles. We certainly must not be very good Christians if we continue to struggle with sin.

Is it any wonder, then, that we can't imagine a God who would give us a sexual ethic that is so pure and exclusive that it often demands suffering in order to live up to it? I cannot have two wives, but I must limit myself to one regardless of what my culture says. We cannot simply live together, enjoying conjugal freedoms like so many in our culture, without first committing ourselves to each other by entering into the covenant of marriage. My marriage must be to a woman and not to another man; the same-sex attraction of my human nature does not invalidate a creation mandate and design. Celibacy is the alternative to marriage's sexual intimacy. And within my marriage, I must be monogamous in my sexual intimacy—this excludes emotional affairs as well as pornographic fantasy.

All of the above is a part of my discipleship and it involves suffering because I must deny what my flesh craves and what my culture views as normative. Yet, it is through suffering, in all of its forms, that I am driven to a deeper trust in a redemptive God who has a purpose for me, and that purpose cannot be found apart from his sanctifying love. He is shaping me to look like Jesus and that process is going to be a painful one because it is antithetical to my sinful human nature. So talk about your struggles and about your pain, because they are a vital part of your discipleship.

"Consider him who endured from sinners such hostility against himself, so that you may not grow weary or fainthearted.

In your struggle against sin you have not yet resisted to the point of shedding your blood. And have you forgotten the exhortation that addresses you as sons? 'My son, do not regard lightly the discipline of the Lord, nor be weary when reproved by him'" (Hebrews 12:3–5).

16

I Am Weak, but Thou . . .

I WANT TO SHARE a page from my journal, which I write in almost every day as a discipline. The practice has helped me track my life and to hold myself more accountable for my own thoughts, attitudes, and behavior. It also helps me to remember people I am praying for, the things that I have read in the Scripture, and the new discoveries of God's truth that I do not want to forget. So many of my sermons and blogs have flowed out this journaling practice. Finally, the practice of journaling has also helped me sift through my feelings and emotions, as well as keeping track of my "progress" with pancreatic cancer, which has been a dominating force in my life since April 2017:

> [A]Sunday, October 20, day thirteen (after eight out of twelve chemo treatments)
> I awoke with the hymn "Guide Me, O Thou Great Jehovah" running through my mind. Listened to it on YouTube. I really do feel like a "pilgrim through this barren land. I am weak but Thou art mighty, guide me with Thy powerful hand . . . Bread of Heaven, feed me till I want no more." Chemo sometimes makes me weepy, and this hymn definitely brought tears to my eyes. I also listened to "It Is Well with My Soul," "Crown Him with Many Crowns," and "I'm No Longer a Slave to Fear." An encouraging time of worship for my sad heart—to bask

in the realization of a good and powerful God, who is my Deliverer.

This reminds me, once again, how my heart responds to songs, hymns, and Scripture that magnify God and describe his greatness and power. I feel safe, like he is my Rock and Fortress; I also feel cared for because he is my strong Father. I remember when one of my boys lost a toy down a storm drain in front of our house. The drain was covered by a very heavy metal grate that I had to deadlift in order for my boy to quickly retrieve his toy. As I was putting the grate back into position, I caught my finger underneath it and yelled in pain as I finally pulled it out. Wow, did that hurt! My boy, who was watching all of this, was horrified—and ran away. He couldn't handle seeing his strong dad hurt.

Another memory comes to mind about how my dad and me used to wrestle when I was a kid. I always admired him for his strength and that he never used it to hurt me. I eventually joined the wrestling team in high school and started to develop physically. The day came when I realized that I could beat my dad, but I continued to let him win when we wrestled. I distinctly remember the thought that I needed my dad to be stronger than me.

I will never have to worry about my Heavenly Father losing strength; I am weak, but he is mighty . . . He is the majestic, all-powerful Creator of the Universe, and he is in control of all things. He is my "Abba," my daddy. He will never use his great strength to hurt me and nothing will ever be able to separate me from his love. My heart overflows with worship . . ."Crown Him the Lord of Years, the Potentate of Time, Creator of the rolling spheres, ineffably sublime. All Hail, Redeemer, Hail! For Thou hast died for me; Thy praise shall never, never fail throughout eternity!"[1]

1. Bridges, "Crown Him with Many Crowns" (1851).

17

Gladly for Aye We Adore Him

ONE OF MY DEAR brothers asked me what my favorite hymn was, and I said, "Praise to the Lord the Almighty," written by Joakim Neander. You may not have heard of him before, but you may have heard of the hymn. The only Joakim we know in these parts is a guy who played for the Chicago Bulls.

Neander was a German poet and hymn writer who lived after the Reformation (sixteenth century). He was also a pastor in the Reformed Church. He wrote sixty hymns and loved to wander among the caves and ravines of a certain valley by the Dussel River. Like many, he was most creative when he was out in God's creation. The valley eventually was named after him—Neander-thal (valley). Sound familiar? This was the very place where the fossilized remains of an early human were found, whom they called Neanderthal Man.

Joakim had been shaped not only by the theology of the Reformation, but also by Pietism and its emphasis on the heart. You can sense the impact of these two influences in his hymns: the majesty of a sovereign God who plans and controls and guides, and the compassion of a God who loves and cares and is worthy of our continual adoration. Joakim left us a significant legacy even though he died at the age of thirty from tuberculosis.

The original hymn had six verses, though only four show up in most hymnals. You can check them out for yourself, but let me point out just a few that have blessed me:

"Praise to the Lord, the Almighty, the King of Creation! O my soul praise Him, for He is thy health and salvation! All ye who hear, now to His temple draw near; praise Him in glad adoration."

Some hear Psalm 150 in this verse. I hear Psalm 103: "Bless the Lord, O my soul, and all that is within me, bless his holy name . . . who forgives all your iniquity and heals all your diseases." Neander wrote "Praise him, for he is thy health and salvation." It makes me wonder how much he struggled with sickness before he eventually succumbed. What a beautiful thought: God is my health.

"Praise to the Lord, who, when tempests their warfare are waging. Who, when the elements madly around thee are raging, biddeth them cease, turneth their fury to peace, whirlwinds and waters assuaging."

"Praise to the Lord, who, when darkness of sin is abounding. Who, when the godless do triumph, all virtue confounding. Sheddeth His light, chaseth the horrors of night, saints with His mercy surrounding."

These last two verses are not usually in the hymnal. What a great hope they give in the face of the darkness and madness raging around us because of human sin. God is in control. He not only restrains evil, but surrounds his saints with mercy. Though we feel overwhelmed, he will chase the darkness away. "When you pass through the waters, I will be with you; and through the rivers they shall not overwhelm you . . ." (Isaiah 43:2).

The last verse is incredible. Imagine a huge pipe organ the size of Texas playing an introduction to this and the voices of million angels and humans singing this slowly and majestically into the darkness of this crappy world: "Praise to the Lord, O let all that is in me adore Him! All that has life and breath, come now with praises before Him. Let the Amen sound from His people again, gladly for aye we adore Him."

Note the very last phrase, "gladly for aye." The word is pronounced "I" and can mean "yes" or "yes sir" (*aye aye*). As an adverb, however, it also means "always, continually, and forever." This is the use of the word here: gladly (delightfully, enthusiastically, willingly, joyfully, passionately) let us forever and always adore *him*! Amen.

18

The Dark Night of the Soul

I JUST FINISHED READING a small, disturbing book written by Elie Wiesel, Holocaust survivor and winner of the 1986 Nobel Peace Prize. *Night* is a chilling tale of his experience in the Auschwitz and Buchenwald concentration camps as a fifteen-year-old. The book is not for the faint of heart because the account of the sheer cruelty of the Nazis is appalling.

Upon his arrival in Birkenau by cattle car, Elie and his father were separated from his mother and sisters, whom they would never see again. The Jews were evaluated to determine whether they should be exterminated or put on the work detail. Elie and his father were deemed fit enough to work, but as they were herded to the prisoners' barracks, they were taken past an open-pit furnace where the Nazis were burning babies by the truckload.

The Jewish arrivals were stripped, shaved, disinfected, and treated with almost unimaginable cruelty. Eventually, their captors marched them from Birkenau to the main camp, Auschwitz. They eventually arrived in Buna, a work camp, where Elie was put to work in an electrical-fittings factory. A vicious foreman forced Elie to give him his gold tooth, which was pried out of his mouth with a rusty spoon. The prisoners were forced to watch the hanging of fellow prisoners in the camp courtyard. On one occasion, the Gestapo even hung an eight-year-old boy who had been associated with some rebels within Buna. Because of the horrific conditions in the camps and the ever-present danger of death, many of the prisoners themselves begin to slide into cruelty, concerned only with personal survival. Sons begin to abandon and abuse their fathers. Elie himself began to lose his humanity and his faith, both in God and in the people around him. I won't tell you any more of the story just in case you want to read the book for yourself.

Behind the physical and emotional struggles, the book revealed the spiritual struggle of this young Jew raised in the Torah and Kabbalah (teachings of Jewish mysticism). For me, the key paragraph in the entire book summed up that struggle:

"Never shall I forget that night, the first night in camp, which has turned my life into one long night . . . Never shall I forget that smoke. Never shall I forget the little faces of the children, whose bodies I saw turned into wreaths of smoke beneath a silent blue sky. Never shall I forget those flames which consumed my faith forever . . . Never shall I forget those moments which murdered my God and my soul and turned my dreams into dust."[1]

He uttered a similar cry when he witnessed the hanging of a little boy who tragically did not die immediately because he was too light for the rope: "For more than an hour he stayed there, struggling between life and death, dying in slow agony under our eyes . . . He was still alive when I passed in front of him. His tongue was still red, his eyes were not glazed. Behind me, I heard a man asking: 'For God's sake, where is God now?' And from within me, I heard a voice answer: 'Where is He? This is where—hanging from the gallows.' That night, the soup tasted like corpses."[2]

How would you answer that question? I am not sure that anyone could at that moment, because the absolute evil of that event would have sucked our breath away. However, eventually you would need to process your experience and help someone else through theirs.

Francois Mauriac, with whom the author became friends later in life, wrote the foreword to the book. Mauriac's words are stunning:

1. Wiesel, *Night*, 34.
2. Wiesel, *Night*, 65.

And I, who believe that God is love, what answer could I give my young questioner, whose dark eyes still held the reflection of that angelic sadness which had appeared one day upon the face of the hanged child? What did I say to him? Did I speak of another Jew, his brother, who may have resembled him—the Crucified, whose Cross has conquered the world? Did I affirm that the stumbling block to his faith was the cornerstone of mine, and that the conformity between the Cross and the suffering of men was in my eyes the key to that impenetrable mystery whereon the faith of his childhood had perished? The Jewish nation has been resurrected from among its thousands of dead. It is through them that it lives again. We do not know the worth of one single drop of blood, one single tear. All is grace. If the Eternal is Eternal, the last word for each one of us belongs to Him.[3]

There are no easy answers to the problem of suffering. However, we believe that at the heart of suffering itself is the *cross*. We also believe that on that cross was "a man of sorrows and acquainted with grief; and as one from whom men hide their faces he was despised, and we esteemed him not. Surely he has borne our griefs and carried our sorrows; yet we esteemed him stricken, smitten by God, and afflicted. But he was pierced for our transgressions; he was crushed for our iniquities; upon him was the chastisement that brought us peace; and with his wounds we are healed" (Isaiah 53:3–5). And the last word for each one of us belongs to him.

3. Wiesel, *Night*, iv.

19

The Laboratory of Suffering

DID YOU HEAR ABOUT the teacher who was helping one of her pupils put on his boots? He asked for help and she could see why. Even with her pulling and him pushing, the little boots still didn't want to go on. By the time they got the second boot on, she had worked up a sweat. She almost cried when the little boy said, "Teacher, they're on the wrong feet." She looked, and sure enough they were. It wasn't any easier pulling the boots off than it was putting them on.

She managed to keep her cool as they worked to get the boots back on, this time on the correct feet. He then announced, "These aren't my boots." She bit her tongue, rather than get right in his face and scream "Why didn't you say so?" like she wanted to. Once again she struggled to help him pull the ill-fitting boots off his little feet.

No sooner had they gotten the boots off did he said, "They're my brother's boots. My mom made me wear 'em." Now she didn't know if she should laugh or cry. But she mustered up what grace and courage she had left to wrestle the boots on his feet again. Helping him into his coat, she asked, "Now, where are your mittens?" He said, "I stuffed 'em in the toes of my boots." I will leave it to your imagination as to what happened next.

A young man once asked Dr. Donald Grey Barnhouse, pastor of the Tenth Presbyterian Church in Philadelphia, if he would pray that God would give the man more patience. Dr. Barnhouse told him, "I will pray that God will give you suffering." The young man was startled and repeated his request. Barnhouse again said that he would pray for God to give him suffering and then explained what he meant by quoting Romans 5:3, ". . . for we know that suffering produces patience [endurance]." Patience is the first thing most of us would admit we need, but the way it is normally achieved is the last thing any of us would want.

Certainly there are those trials which come upon us that leave us numb and bloodied—the death of a loved one, or a tragedy out of the twilight zone. As I write this I am thinking of a wonderful family in Massachusetts whose oldest daughter had been in a coma for several weeks due to viral meningitis and eventually passed away. I am also thinking of the great sadness experienced by the family of one of my college roommates who died on Christmas day. They each learned patient endurance as they hung on to their God and his goodness through their tears.

For many, however, their laboratory of suffering is more akin to a mitten in the toe of a boot by comparison—the annoying people at work or school, a selfish spouse, ungrateful kids, demanding parents, or the frustrating people in church who don't see things the way we do. All of these situations are also the petri dishes in which patient endurance grows and develops. Why? Because God uses these situations to show us that everyone else is wrong and we are right, so we have to develop patience in order to live with these yahoos? I don't think so. Rather, God uses these situations to show us our own loveless and selfish hearts so that we will humble ourselves before him, repent, and trust his grace and mercy to change us to be more like Jesus. That is why Paul finishes his thought in Romans 5:3–4 by saying, ". . . for we know that suffering produces endurance [patience]; and endurance produces character, and character produces hope, and hope does not put us to shame, because God's love has been poured into our hearts through the Holy Spirit, who has been given to us."

20

God Is Our Refuge

God is our refuge and strength; a very present help in trouble. Therefore, we will not fear though the earth gives way, though the mountains be moved into the heart of the sea, though its waters roar and foam, though the mountains tremble at its swelling. (Psalm 46:1–3. This text was the basis and inspiration for Martin Luther's famous hymn *Ein Feste Burg Ist Unser Got*, "A Mighty Castle [Fortress] Is Our God.")

FROM THE PAGES OF the Old Testament to the New, we are told: *fear not; don't be afraid or dismayed; do not fear; let not your heart be troubled.* Fear should have no place in the life of the believer because it takes God out of the picture and places the situation completely under our control. If we are afraid of something, it is at that point of our lives that we have eliminated God. That is why fear is usually accompanied by anxiety and despair, because we are overwhelmed by what we are facing, because we are facing it alone. Fear eats away at our confidence and distorts our understanding of God. It is therefore essential to learn that the opposite of fear is not courage to stand up against impossible circumstances, but faith and trust in a sovereign God who has all things under his control, and whose plans for us as his children are never for evil, but always to give us a future and a hope.

The Heidelberg Catechism is instructive here: "We can be patient when things go against us, thankful when things go well, and for the future we can have good confidence in our faithful God and Father that nothing will separate us from his love. All creatures are so completely in his hand that without his will they can neither move or be moved."[1]

1. *Heidelberg Catechism*, 19.

21

Fear Not, Little Flock

So, WHERE IS YOUR anxiety level these days? Level orange? Our culture of fear has provided lots of munchies to feed our fear monsters: terrorism, angry and unstable people (could be that neighbor who seems normal but keeps to himself) committing acts of violence, an erratic North Korea, a desperate Iran, Russian involvement in U.S. politics, the confusion of our whole political system, and unequal system of justice for African-Americans, the future of healthcare, the debt-ridden economy of Illinois, West Nile virus, Ebola, SARS, H1N1 . . . do you remember these last ones? Now there is COVID-19.

I will spare you the statistics of this present virus and say that while it is very serious, by taking proper precautions (and listening to people who know what they are talking about) we can mitigate the worst-case scenarios that the media is suggesting. Mysterious diseases, political intrigue, and acts of violence and terrorism make big stories, and media hype tends to report the reality disproportionately. If you still watch the evening news on TV, you almost need a sedative afterwards. Such news feeds our fears and diverts our attention from dealing with present issues and concerns, as well as seeing present opportunities for the gospel.

In *Break Open the Sky*, Stephan Bauman (former president of World Relief) says,

Faith, it seems, has a branding problem. Meanwhile, anxiety in the US has reached epidemic levels . . . Fear is popular today because it's profitable. Producers of media in all its forms have become merchants of fear, stoking fires of controversy, threat, or anger in search of larger audiences. Politicians, both conservative and progressive, traffic in fear to secure support and shore up votes. Corporations employ fear to make us buy more of their products. Friends warn us of the latest health scare, food allergy, or crime epidemic. Even religion, as an enterprise, makes use of fear.[1]

We Americans are experts at trying to control our own lives. We are self-sufficient and we tend to provide for ourselves quite well, thank you! We reduce our risks to the minimum, fix all our own problems, and anticipate all eventualities—well, at least we try. When something comes along, like a new virus for which no antidote yet exists and which threatens our economy, we feel helpless, frustrated, and out of control—a feeling that Americans hate. We also start to connect our present fear to all the rest in our anxiety arsenal and overwhelm ourselves with worry and precaution and a bit of paranoia.

Earlier Christians (and many in the Majority World today)[2] lived in unsafe and hostile societies that were vulnerable to constant war, natural disasters without warning, and real incurable diseases. They had little control over their lives and had little sense of a bright earthly future. However, they did have faith in a God who never forgets the cross and would never forget them. *Their antidote to fear was not an inoculation, but trust in a sovereign and loving God who has all things under control.*

When the prophet Habakkuk looked at his uncertain future, he was overcome with fear. However, he did not allow this fear to paralyze him and he chose to do two things: focus on the character of God, who never changes (1:12), and then listen to God's word

1. Bauman, *Break Open the Sky*, 2.

2. In an essay titled "The Epidemic of Worry" David Brooks wrote, "According to the World Health Organization, 18.2% of Americans report chronic anxiety while only 3.3% of Nigerians."

to quell his fear. "The just shall live by his faith" (2:4). *The antidote for fear is not courage but faith.*

So if we really want to listen to a sovereign God who never changes, then we must begin by hearing the consistent message spoken to the people under the old covenant and to those of us under the new: **Do not be afraid!**

I will not list all these passages but will mention one found in Luke 12:32, where Jesus told his disciples, "Fear not, little flock, for it is the Father's good pleasure to give you the kingdom." I wish I had a visual of Jesus speaking to this insignificant little band of wide-eyed men who were ready to be sent out into a violent world to spread the gospel, with a few provisions and seemingly little hope of success. And yet Jesus said (my paraphrase), *My little flock—those who are my special ones under my care, whom I love— FEAR NOT! The reason not to fear is because your Father is absolutely delighted to give you a future, the very kingdom that you are being sent out to share with others will be your eternal inheritance. And since he will bestow upon you a future glory that you cannot imagine, you do not need to worry that he will provide everything you need in this life as you risk it for his kingdom.*

Apparently, I am included in the most vulnerable-to-the-virus category because I am over sixty-five, receiving treatment for cancer, and have diabetes. Yet, I am convinced that there is nothing that will come to me (or you) that has not first passed through the hand of our Heavenly Father and is designed to make us more like Jesus. FEAR NOT . . .

22

God's Comfort in Your Affliction

WHAT DOES IT MEAN to experience the comfort of God when we are facing trouble or affliction? Think about that before we move on . . . What does God's comfort feel like to you? For me, as I have faced some dark times in my wrestling match with pancreatic cancer, God's comfort has often come as a freedom from fear through trusting in his providential care. God's comfort has also shown itself by an awareness of his presence and the overwhelming sense of peace that such an awareness brings. It is like my soul says, "God's got this, bro. Go have a good meal!"

The Lord has also comforted me through the care and encouragement of others—their prayers, cards, letters, emails, texts, just letting me know they were thinking about me or praying for me. I remember when I was guest-preaching at a church and a group of about twenty people gathered around me after the service to pray for me—guess my sermon was really bad (just kidding). They laid hands on me and prayed for my healing and spiritual well-being.

In another church, a smaller one, the *entire congregation* prayed for me just before I gave the benediction. I could give you example after example of how God has used others to comfort and encourage me—like many of you reading this post. Thus, when Paul in 2 Corinthians 1:4 calls God "the Father of mercies and the God of all comfort, who comforts us in all our affliction," I understand what that means, because he has comforted me and continues to do so.

However, that is not all Paul says about God's comfort. In verse 4, he continues: "who comforts us in our affliction, *so that* we can comfort those who are in any affliction, with the comfort with which we ourselves are comforted by God." This reminds me of Psalm 67, where the psalmist asks that God would bless and be gracious to him and his people, "*so that* your way may be known on the earth and your saving power among all nations." God blesses us *so that* we can bring the blessings of the gospel to others.

And so it is with all of God's gifts; they do not stop with us. We are to love others "as I have loved you" (John 13:14); we are to forgive one another "as God in Christ has forgiven you" (Ephesians 4:32); we are to be generous in the use of our wealth, because "we know the grace of our Lord Jesus Christ, that though he was rich, yet for your sake he became poor, so that you by his poverty might become rich" (2 Corinthians 8:9). Therefore, God's comfort is not designed to make us comfortable, but to make us a comfort to others, like some of the examples I gave above.

There is one more thing that Paul says about comfort in 2 Corinthians 1:6: "If we are afflicted, it is for your comfort and salvation; and if we are comforted, it is for your comfort, which you experience when you patiently endure the same sufferings that we suffer." It seems like Paul is saying that whatever trouble or affliction he suffered would have an impact upon others and produce in them patient endurance when they suffered.

I remember that soon after my diagnosis I initially did not want a lot of people to know I had cancer. It was humbling to admit and it made me feel weak and vulnerable. My oldest daughter sensed my hesitation and challenged me to let people know, so they could be praying for me. Then she said (at least this is what I remember), "Dad, we are going to be watching you, because how you handle all of this is going to set a pattern for your children and grandchildren." The same thought was expressed to me by two other people in my church; they were watching how I was handling all this and they expressed how important it was to their faith.

What a powerful thing to recognize that our afflictions do not take place in a vacuum. Other people are drawn in and are affected directly or indirectly by what we suffer. To personalize this: I know that I do not suffer alone (although sometimes I feel that way when I'm having a pity party). There are more people than I can imagine who have been pulled into my world through kinship, friendship, and "virtual" relationship who are impacted by my affliction. And that is true for you as well. How you deal with your troubles can bring tremendous comfort to others whose faith is untested in certain areas.

It can be a great encouragement to their faith to see an example of someone who is not embittered against the Lord or constantly whining about the hand s/he's been dealt. Instead, they see on display a very ordinary human being, simply trusting, hoping, and enduring because s/he believes that God is good, in control, and will never leave nor forsake them. I guarantee that such an example will be of inestimable value in their spiritual development and will strengthen the muscles of their faith, especially to have the privilege of praying for you during your affliction. Do not be afraid of letting people know of your need, which is very humbling at first, but after a while becomes very freeing. Not only that, but God will bring you comfort and healing through those prayers. God's comfort comes full circle back to you.

So, if you are suffering affliction today, may you experience the comfort that only the God of All Comfort can give to you. May you also look for those within your sphere of influence whom you can comfort in some way with the comfort you have received from God. Finally, may you recognize that, though you wish for anonymity in your suffering, you are on display before family and friends, who will be greatly influenced by your simple faith and trust in the Father. Let them know how they can be praying for you and allow yourself to receive the comfort and blessing that it will bring.

23

The Man with the Shriveled Hand

I HAVE ALWAYS BEEN intrigued with the account in Matthew 12:9–14 of the man with the shriveled hand. I believe that this whole scenario was a setup by the Pharisees (Luke 6:7–8). These religious leaders were in the process of garnering evidence so that they might bring charges against Jesus for breaking the Law of Moses. I believe they positioned this poor man in the temple on the Sabbath just to see what Jesus would do. Actually, they knew what he would do—Jesus would heal the man and the trap would be sprung.

It shows how callous these Pharisees had become in their interpretation of the Law.[1] Earlier in Matthew 12, the Pharisees had criticized Jesus' hungry disciples for picking grain to eat from the edges of a field on the Sabbath. Jesus responded to this criticism by cutting through the fog of oral tradition by establishing two important principles based upon the original purpose of the Law:

---

1. It was originally passed on to them as oral tradition and ultimately written down in the third century AD as the Mishnah, containing sixty-three tractates on various subjects—eight hundred pages in English. Later, the Jews began to interpret these interpretations in commentaries called the Talmud; the Jerusalem Talmud had twelve volumes and the Babylonian Talmud sixty volumes.

1. The Sabbath was made for man (for his rest and well-being) and not man for the Sabbath.

2. God desires mercy and not sacrifice (Hosea 6:6).

These religious leaders used this man as a pawn to achieve their own malicious goal of doing away with Jesus. By considering his healing on the Sabbath unlawful according to their oral tradition, the Pharisees treated this man with less mercy than they would show one of their own farm animals. In Deuteronomy 22:4 the Law of Moses makes provision to allow the rescue of such an animal if it falls into a ditch on the Sabbath. Yet these super-spiritual, merciless leaders, by their own interpretation of the Law, did not allow the rescue of this man made in the image of God. This made Jesus angry.

Jesus showed the man mercy and established the man's dignity as an image-bearer of God by healing him. However, it was *how* Jesus healed this man that intrigues me and teaches me one more aspect in understanding the word *faith*. Jesus told the man, "Stretch out your hand." Think about that—Jesus did not "unwither" the man's hand first and then tell him to stretch it out. He told him to stretch out his shriveled hand—the very thing he could not do. The man could have said, "Lord, why do you think they call me the man with the withered hand? I can't stretch it out! I need you to heal it first." Instead, as this man acted upon the word of Christ, he received the ability to do what he could not do and was healed.

Faith, then, is acting upon the specific word of Christ and in so doing finding the ability to do what we cannot do in our own strength. Let me give an example of how this might look. I'm sitting next to someone on an airplane and sense that God wants me to engage my seatmate in conversation that may lead to sharing the gospel. So I pray that God will give me strength and wisdom to do that. And then I wait for "power from on high," for God to give me an anointing for witness—change me from Clark Kent into Super-Dave. That would be nice, but it has rarely happened to me. Instead, I usually start engaging my seatmate and trust that God will work through the process.

So, "stretch out your hand"; start the conversation, give that gift, ask to pray for that needy one, be merciful to your enemy, love the unlovely one, don't be anxious at bad news—whatever you cannot do in your own strength, trust in the word of Christ and "stretch out your hand." And watch how the Holy Spirit shows up.

24

More Thoughts on Faith

I WAS READING THE other morning about Jesus' ministry in his hometown of Nazareth as recorded for us in Mark 6:1–6. The townspeople marveled at his wisdom and teaching, and yet they apparently did not believe that he was the Messiah because they knew him and his family. *He grew up here; we've known him since he was a kid and we've known his brothers and sisters. He certainly has gotten a good education somewhere, but he's just one of us. Who does he think he is, getting off acting like the Messiah?* They were scandalized by him. Jesus responded by saying, "A prophet is not without honor, except in his own hometown and among his relatives and in his own household." And consequently "he could do no mighty work there . . . because of their unbelief." However, the text goes on to add, "except that he laid hands on a few sick people and healed them."

What are we to make of this? Is it true that God can only work where there is enough faith, and if he does not work does it show that the faith that is present doesn't measure up?" Many years ago, during a serious back injury that sidelined me for three months, someone came to my house to pray for me. This person told me that if someone prayed for my healing and yet I remained bedridden, it was because I did not have enough faith. And God can't work where there is no faith.

This was not an encouragement to me. How much faith is needed before God can work? Is there a barometer in heaven that has a baseline for the amount of faith we must have before God answers prayer? I have always found solace in the words of Jesus that even if we have faith the size of a tiny mustard seed, we can move mountains. I'm not sure what that means, but apparently it doesn't take hyper-faith to be the default setting for God to work. The problem at Nazareth was not a "little faith" but "no faith," which stemmed from stubborn unbelief.

One commentator that I was reading intimated that this passage teaches us that there are certain situations where we can actually tie God's hands because of our lack of faith. I strongly disagree. Our faith, or the lack of it, does not rule God. I do not believe that this is the lesson of Mark 6:1–6. Instead, I believe that among the lessons of this text is that familiarity with the messenger can often interfere with accepting the message. (Sometimes the hardest people to reach are those in our own family.) The text also teaches that God works where he wills; in most cases he chooses to work in response to our faith, but sometimes he chooses to work where there is no faith in order to produce faith in hearts filled with unbelief.

We see elsewhere in Mark that a person's faith was not necessary for a miracle (1:31). We also see that sometimes it was the faith of friends and family that was recognized (2:5; 7:32). At other times (9:24) it was a matter of "Lord I believe, help my unbelief." Even in this little town of "no faith" (Nazareth), God chose to heal some who were sick.

Faith is not a commodity we offer God in order to merit a hearing. Rather, faith is a position that we adopt wherein we choose to trust God and submit to his will for us no matter the circumstances. No sincere child of God should ever be judged for a lack of faith just because they do not receive that for which they ask—they are probably hurting enough as it is. Instead, they should be encouraged to trust in the Lord with all their heart, even in the midst of God's silence (Mark 7:26; Matthew 15:23). It is in this position of trust alone that they will find the growth of a deeper dependency on their Heavenly Father and a greater usefulness in his kingdom because they have learned how to persevere (James 1:3).

25

Even More Thoughts on Faith

I AM SITTING HERE drinking barium and waiting in the doctor's office to get a CT scan that will reveal what impact the twelve treatments of chemotherapy I just completed have had on my pancreatic cancer. As I was praying, I was reminded of Jesus' Gethsemane prayer in Matthew 26: ". . . nevertheless, not my will but yours be done." If Jesus were to pray this prayer today as a member of the "hyper-faith" movement, he might have said, "Father, by the authority given to me as your beloved Son, I claim the victory in advance over this coming crucifixion! In your name, I command that the forces of evil be defeated and that this cup of suffering be taken away from me! Vindicate me according to my faith."

Instead, what we hear from the lips of our Lord is an agonizing prayer that would not cut it in a more charismatic gathering. "My Father, if it is possible . . ." (Matthew); "everything is possible for you" (Mark); "if you are willing" (Luke), "take this cup from me. Yet, not as I will, but as you will." The bottom line for Jesus was to do the will of God, not to escape his pain. It is faintly reminiscent of the faith statement of Daniel's three friends who were threatened with death in the fiery furnace if they did not bow down to Nebuchadnezzar's golden image. "If this be so, our God whom we serve is able to deliver us from the burning fiery furnace, and he will deliver us out of your hand, O King. But if not [if he is not willing], be it known to you, O King, that we will not serve your gods or worship the golden image that you have set up" (Daniel 3:17–18).

Do you honestly think that such a prayer made by Jesus and the confessional by Daniel's friends demonstrate a lack of faith? There are some who would claim so—that praying for God's will to be done is a default position that shows a shallow faith. I once heard a TV evangelist say, "For those who do not have the faith to boldly ask God for something, they always tend to meekly ask him for his will to be done." Really?

I believe that such a perspective shows how Satan can twist Scripture (for example, the temptation of Jesus in the wilderness) in order to sow seeds of confusion and disagreement among God's people—all under the guise of super-spirituality. It reminds me of the teaching of the Pharisees, whose twisted interpretation of the Law kept God's people in bondage.

What has been helpful for me to think through this issue of faith and God's will is the analogy that Jesus drew between the good gifts our Father desires to give us as his children and those we wish to bestow on our own children. "If you then, who are evil [not a perfect parent like God], know how to give good gifts to your children, how much more will your Heavenly Father give good things to those who ask him!" (Matthew 7:11). The context is that Jesus was encouraging his followers to continue to ask, seek, and knock for things they desired from God.

Let's say your older child comes to you and presents a request in this way: "Dad [Mom], on the basis of the authority you have given me as your beloved child, I claim in advance the right to be given $450 of my future inheritance in order to pay for the repairs on my car!" Do you have any initial reactions to this scenario?

However, let's say your child comes to you in this way: "Dad [Mom], I know that it is possible for you to take away the burden of my car repair bill. I also know that you love me and know what is best for me, so I trust you to do what is according to your will because what you want for me is more important than what I want for myself." After you pick yourself up from off the floor, how would you respond to this request? Which request demonstrates the greatest amount of trust in you?

How much more your Heavenly Father . . .

26

Lord, Teach Us to Number Our Days

Lord, you have been our dwelling place in all generations. Before the mountains were brought forth, or ever you had formed the earth and the world, from everlasting to everlasting you are God. You return man to dust and say, "Return, O children of man!" For a thousand years in your sight are but as yesterday when it is past, or as a watch in the night. You sweep them away as with a flood; they are like a dream, like grass that is renewed in the morning: in the morning it flourishes and is renewed; in the evening it fades and withers. For we are brought to an end by your anger; by your wrath we are dismayed. You have set our iniquities before you, our secret sins in the light of your presence. For all our days pass away under your wrath; we bring our years to an end like a sigh. The years of our life are seventy, or even by reason of strength eighty; yet their span is but toil and trouble; they are soon gone, and we fly away. Who considers the power of your anger, and your wrath according to the fear of you? So teach us to number our days that we may get a heart of wisdom. (Psalm 90:1–12)

MOSES HERE ACKNOWLEDGES THAT there is something terribly wrong in the world because we who were the crown of God's creation are fallen and finite creatures. Our lives are short and filled with trouble, and our death is inevitable. In the face of this inevitability, Moses prays, "... *teach us to number our days that we may get a heart of wisdom.*" We must learn to number our days properly so that we can live our lives wisely.

Let me give you a few things to ponder that will go a long way in helping us to live wisely. I am only going to name a few things; they are simple and pastoral, and yet incredibly important. I would invite you to add to the list and teach them to your children.

- *Make sure that those closest to you know that you love them.* In fact, today is the day to learn to say, "I love you," and to say it regularly. These are the most profound words you could leave as a legacy to your loved ones. Many a child has grown to adulthood and been left with words such as "You'll never amount to anything" or "You're a mistake; we never really wanted you." Many a wife or husband has been left wondering if she/he was really loved. And so, one of the ways to create a wise and lasting positive legacy is to make sure your loved ones know you love them. Today is the day to begin; say it, don't assume it.

- *Make sure that you keep short accounts.* Today is the day to learn to say, "I'm sorry," and to say it often. Grudges are built up over time; unforgiveness turns to bitterness and to resentment; unreconciled relationships separate us and can be passed on to future generations. How many of the world conflicts today find their root in generational grudges and tribal revenge? And how many issues in our families are rooted in the hearts of people who refuse to forgive and seek reconciliation?—until it's too late, and all they have left is regret. You do not always have to be right, but you should always be sorry. It is hard to die in peace when you are overcome with regret. It is not too late to begin to wisely learn to say, "I'm sorry."

- *Make sure that you have thought deeply about where you will be ten seconds after you die.* Today is the day to get right with God. Since death is inevitable and we will all someday face our Maker, are you prepared? "I'll deal with that when it comes," but you do not know when it will come, do you? I was talking to an old guy (older than me, so he was really old) two summers ago who wasn't sure he believed in God, but he said, "If there is a God, then he'll know that I've done the best I could—he'll understand." I told him that the problem is that our best isn't good enough and God doesn't grade on the curve. He demands perfection, which eliminates all of us from contention. "All have sinned and fall short of the glory of God" (Romans 3:23). This is why we need a Savior. The old gentleman looked at me with a little smile on his face and said, "Hmm, well, I'll take my chances." He's right; he is taking a big chance . . . not wise!

Remember the 2004 Mel Gibson movie, *The Passion of the Christ?* The trailer was simply a dark screen with these words: "He was wounded for our transgressions, he was crushed for our iniquities . . ." This is a verse from Isaiah 53 and it continues: ". . . upon him was the chastisement that brought us peace and with his stripes we are healed. All we like sheep have gone astray . . ." Our Messiah took our sins upon himself so that we could be forgiven and reconciled to God. Therefore, it is the one who believes in Jesus Christ and what he has done on the cross who is ready face life and death and to stand before God without fear . . . very wise.

"No guilt in life, no fear in death, this is the pow'r of Christ in me; from life's first cry to final breath, Jesus commands my destiny. No pow'r of hell, no scheme of man, can ever pluck me from his hand; till he returns or takes me home, here in the pow'r of Christ I'll stand."[1]

A story is told of a note found by the bedside of a young man who had died after a brief illness: "What shall I think when I am called to die? Shall I not find too soon my life has ended? The

---

1. Townend, "In Christ Alone."

years, too quickly, have hastened by with so little done of all that I'd intended. There were so many things I'd meant to try, so many contests I'd hoped to win, and now the end approaches just as I was thinking of preparing to begin."[2]

Lord, teach me to number my days . . .

---

2. Author and source unknown.

27

The Silence of God

FORTY-FIVE YEARS AGO I preached a sermon on the silence of God. After three years of pastoral ministry under my belt I came to the conclusion that God's silence is never due to indifference, but always to higher thoughts or greater purposes. "'For as the heavens are higher than the earth, so are my ways higher than your ways and my thoughts than your thoughts, says the Lord'" (Isaiah 55:9). Not a bad conclusion for a young greenhorn pastor who was trying to be faithful to God's Word without a lot of experience in applying it.

Today, after forty-eight years of pastoral ministry experience, I am still and will always remain a greenhorn at trying to figure out the ways of an eternal God. I still believe that God's silence is one of a higher purpose, but I would state it differently now. I would say, *God is never silent*. We could cite Psalm 19, where we read that the heavens are declaring the glory of God—that God is speaking in creation, loud enough to hold us accountable for not believing that he exists (Romans 1:18–20). Also, we could go to Hebrews and read that God has spoken in the past through the prophets, ". . . but in these last days he has spoken through his Son, Jesus, the Word of God" (Hebrews 1:2).

That God is never silent can also be seen from the few notable occasions in the Gospels when Jesus was silent in the present of someone. He was silent when the Canaanite woman asked him to heal her daughter (Matthew 15:21–28). He was silent before Caiaphas and the Sanhedrin at the kangaroo court hastily convened to accuse him of blasphemy on trumped-up charges (Matthew 26:59–63). He was also silent before Herod, who saw him as a bit of a curiosity (Luke 23:9).

I would submit to you that in each of these situations Jesus was shouting in his "silence." To Herod, whose only interest was to see Jesus walk across his swimming pool (if you are familiar with the rock opera *Jesus Christ Super Star)*, Jesus was shouting, "I will not be trivialized!" His "silence" was a judgment against the spiritual shallowness of Herod. His "silence" before the Sanhedrin was a shout against their spiritual hypocrisy and their self-interest in preserving their own place and ambitions. Finally, in his "silence" before the Canaanite woman he was shouting out, "Trust me, trust me!" He was drawing out of her a faith born of desperation. She knew who he was and had heard of his compassion, and so in the face of his "silence" she cast herself upon his mercy and said, "Lord help me!"

We find a parallel between the "silence" this woman confronted and the greatest silence in all of Scripture; the silence of the cross. In that silence, Jesus himself cried out, "My God, my God, why have you forsaken me?" (Matthew 27:46). In that silence, the disciples ran away and the women were in despair. And yet . . . and yet . . . just a few days later it became clear that in the midst of this great "silence" God was doing his greatest work. In the silence, God was shouting, "I love you!"

Helmut Theilicke wrote a book titled *The Silence of God* at the height of the darkness of World War II. In it he said this: "Even when we thought He did not care, or was dead, He knew all about us and behind the dark wings He did His work of love. We live in the power of this Golgotha night of silence. Where should we be without the cross?"[1]

Thus, as we face the life-dominating issues that seem to render silent God's voice, let us hold on to the theology of the cross.

1. Theilicke, *Silence of God*, 14–15.

Let us remember that even in his silence God is not silent—he is speaking, he is working, he is fulfilling his higher purposes of a grander plan than we can ever imagine. He is shouting for us to trust him because he loves us.

He who has ears to hear, let him listen!

28

Pandemics and the Throne of God

I HAVE FINALLY FINISHED the book of Revelation in my latest read-through of the Bible. To say that Revelation is hard to interpret is about as obvious as saying that an elephant is a rather large animal. However, while it may be difficult, it is not impossible and it is worth the study. Do not get bogged down with the specifics of the symbolism or in trying to chart the chronology. Also, make sure you are trying to understand it as if you are reading it in the first century, not the twenty-first. And I have found it helpful to see that chapters 4 and 5 are the watershed of the entire book.

If you have a chance, read these chapters. I have preached on them many times because they outline key components of worship. However, narrowing the focus of this passage just to worship can obscure it from its key position in John's vision. And the purpose of this vision is to show us, in beautiful symbolism, that all things are governed by the "Throne-Occupant."[1] The phrase *the throne* or *God's throne* (occurs seventeen times in these chapters) is at the very center of the universe and its presence precedes all of the symbolic description of the trials and tribulations that will follow.

The throne represents sovereignty, indicating that nothing can take place apart from the providential hand of God. Linger by

1. Hendriksen, *More Than Conquerors*, 101.

the throne in chapter 4, along with the all-seeing Holy Spirit[2] (the seven blazing lamps), and with the cherubim, who can do nothing other than to gaze upon the glory of God the Father and God the Holy Spirit. They never stop singing his praises, along with redeemed humanity represented by the twenty-four elders, who worship him and lay all their achievements before his throne.

In chapter 5, John sees a sealed scroll that no one can open, and he weeps. The scroll is the "unrevealed and unexecuted" plan of God for human history,[3] and unless it is opened this plan will not be carried out and will remain unfulfilled. The world will be out of control and evil will have its way. Then John's attention is drawn by a redeemed one (an elder) to the Lion of the tribe of Judah (the kingly tribe), who also looks like a slaughtered lamb. It is Jesus Christ, who takes the scroll in his role as mediator[4] and opens it by the power of his indestructible life—his death and resurrection. He is the only one in the entire universe worthy to do so. He then is enthroned. He takes his seat upon the throne beside the Father, so that it now becomes "the throne of God and of the Lamb" (Revelation 22:1, 3). From the throne, Christ the King mediates and executes the plan of God for all of human history and for the church.

As soon as the King is enthroned, there is a burst of enthusiasm with three separate doxologies. Now heaven is ready; now the universe is ready; now the church is ready—Christ is on the throne. Let the trials begin, let the wars wage, let the pandemics rage—we know that they will end in victory by the Lamb who was slain! Follow the book all the way to the end and you will see that the throne becomes the great white throne of judgment, before which the books will be opened and anyone whose name is not found written in the book of life will be thrown into the lake of fire

---

2. Hendriksen, *More Than Conquerors*, 105.

3. Hendriken, *More Than Conquerors*, 108.

4. Note the song in Revelation 5:9 declaring that the Lamb is worthy to open the seals because he was slain and that "by your blood you ransomed people for God."

(20:11–15). And follow it further still and you will hear the one seated on the throne say, "I am making everything new" (21:5).

So, my friend, the key to interpreting Revelation is not to begin with the pandemics and famine, the horses and battles, the Gogs and Magogs, the mark of the beast and 666—but with the throne of God. Likewise, the key to understanding human history is to start at the same place; not with your present circumstances, your fear, or even your suffering; but with Jesus, our King and Savior, on the throne, executing our Father's plan for those who are his (Romans 8:33–34). Do you belong to him?

29

Preparing for Your Exodus or Playing the Fool

ONE OF THE MOST fascinating descriptions of the death of a believer is that of an *exodus* or *departure*. Paul said of his competing desires of continuing to live and minister juxtaposed to wanting to go home to be with the Lord, "I am hard pressed between the two. My desire to *depart* and be with Christ, for that is far better. But to remain in the flesh is more necessary on your account" (Philippians 1:23–24). On the Mount of Transfiguration, Jesus spoke of his impending death as an *exodus*, a *departure* (Luke 9:31). And Peter wanted his brothers to remember his words after his *departure* (2 Peter 1:15). So the Christian should view her/his death not as the end, but as the beginning of a journey to a land of promise and rest that God has prepared for his children.

There was a story told of a king who had in his court a jester (also called the *court fool*) whom he would call upon to make him laugh and lighten his heart when discouraged. During one visit, the king laughed so much that he exclaimed, "Jester, I am going to give you my scepter and I want you to search my kingdom for a fool greater than yourself." So, the jester spent months scouring the kingdom for one who would be more of a fool than he was. He traveled far and wide and could find no one. Finally, he received word to report back the castle because the king was on his death-bed. He sat beside the dying king, who sadly told the him that he was going on a long journey from which he would never return. The jester responded, "Sire, where will this journey take you?" The king said, "I don't know." The jester then asked, "Your Majesty, are you prepared for this journey?" The king quietly replied, "No, I don't even know how to prepare." The jester then took the king's scepter that he had been carrying all these months and gave it to the king, for he had finally found a fool greater than himself.

There is truth here that if death is a journey, then we should know where we are going and how to prepare for the trip. If we know Jesus Christ as our Savior and Lord, then we know that this journey will lead to the eternal kingdom of heaven. He has already gone on ahead of us as the "pioneer of our salvation" (Hebrews 2:10) to prepare a place for us in his Father's house (John 14:2–3). What a wonderful hope! In God's house there is a place for us; a place of belonging because we are in the family of God. Do you have that hope? Do you trust in Christ alone as your entry way to heaven? Or are you unsure of where you stand with God and whether you will be accepted into heaven? Do not be a fool and come to the end of your life unprepared for the journey.

The first part of preparing for your exodus is to know where you are going. The second part is to let people know that you know where you are going. You may have a will, a healthcare proxy, a DNR, and you are an organ donor, but have you prepared your funeral or memorial service? I do not mean printing up the bulletin at Staples complete with the order of worship. Have you written down some of your favorite passages of Scripture that you would like read, or suggested some of your favorite songs you would like sung? Doing this will be of great help to your family as they will be the ones who print up the bulletin.

Finally, have you thought of writing out a statement that could be read to the congregation by the pastor/priest or one of your family members? This statement can be a powerful witness to your faith in Christ and the certainty of your hope of eternal life. Do not make it long and do not make it mysterious, like, "If you are listening to this message, then you will know that I'm dead." Just make it a simple statement of your love for your family and of your hope in Jesus. It can be powerful.

I will finish with two such statements. The first was written by Jonathan Edwards, American pastor and theologian, five years before his death:

> First of all, I give and commend my soul into the hands of God that gives it, and to the Lord Jesus Christ its glorious, all sufficient, faithful and chosen Redeemer, relying alone on the free and infinite mercy and grace of God through his worthiness and mediation, for its eternal salvation; and my body I commend to the earth, to be committed to the dust in Christian burial . . . hoping through the grace, faithfulness, and almighty power of my everlasting Redeemer, to receive the same again, at the last day, made like unto his glorious body.[1]

This second statement was part of the last will and testament of John Newton, the old converted slave trader and author of the hymn "Amazing Grace":

> I commit my soul to my gracious God and Saviour, who mercifully spared and preserved me, when I was an apostate, a blasphemer, and an infidel, and delivered me from that state of misery on the coast of Africa into which my obstinate wickedness had plunged me and who has been pleased to admit me (though most unworthy) to preach His glorious Gospel. I rely with humble confidence upon the atonement and mediation of the Lord Jesus Christ, God and Man, which I have often proposed to others as the only Foundation whereon a sinner can build His hope, trusting that He will guard and guide me through the uncertain remainder of my life, and that He will then admit me into His presence in His heavenly kingdom.[2]

1. Murray, *Jonathan Edwards*, 422.
2. Cecil, *Works of John Newton's*, 90–91.

30

Negotiating with God

I AM SITTING IN a dark room in the hospital waiting for a PET scan, after being injected with radioactive dye. This scan will literally light up all the areas of my body that are infected by cancer. It will give a definitive view of where I am at after three years of living with this disease. Sometimes it is hard to know what to pray for at times like this. There is the human tendency to want to negotiate with God. "Lord, could you give me five more years . . . how about three . . . maybe two?" Is it wrong to do this? I guess it all depends on if, in the end, we are willing to accept God's answer.

Abraham is an example of someone who negotiated with God in prayer. In Genesis 19, we see the angel of Lord telling Abraham that he is about ready to destroy the city of Sodom because of its great wickedness. Abe is alarmed because his nephew Lot and family are living there. So he begins to negotiate with God about the baseline number of righteous people there would need to be living in Sodom before the Lord would stay his hand of judgment. Abraham starts high with fifty people: *Just fifty people, Lord—is that too much to ask for you to stay your hand of judgment?* God "relents" and is willing to reconsider all the way down to ten people—sounds like an Amish auction! It seems like God just cannot make up his mind and Abraham is setting the agenda for prayer. Certain theologians and others who struggle with God's sovereignty love this, because it seems to show that while God has a plan, it is set in wet cement, allowing for input and adjustments.

Then the negotiations suddenly end, the angel of the Lord departs, and it is all over for Sodom. Why? What is going on here—why didn't Abraham keep negotiating down to four people (Lot and his wife and their two daughters)? There were at least four righteous ones, right? Wait a minute, only four? Aha . . . then the light bulb moment. Abraham comes around to realize what God is doing. He thinks: *Now I realize that Sodom really is wicked—only four righteous ones in the whole town, and they don't even belong there, because they are my family. That city really does deserve judgment and God is perfectly just in destroying it!*

Thus, what initially looked like God relenting or changing his mind turned out to be a way of bringing Abraham around to his way of thinking. We see a similar strategy (for an opposite reason) that God used with Jonah after Nineveh was spared judgment, and Jonah was beside himself with anger because God showed mercy. God grew up a plant to offer shade from the burning sun while the sulking prophet just sat there waiting for God to come around to his way of thinking. Then God used a little worm to destroy the plant, which made Jonah angry, but showed him that he was more concerned for his own comfort than he was for the thousands in Nineveh who had just repented.

Someone once said that Jonah waited beneath the comfort of his shade plant for God to come around to his way of *thinking*, while God destroyed Jonah's comfort and waited for him to come around to his (God's) way of *loving*.

We tend to look at prayer as a way of getting things from God—and we are enjoined to ask, seek, and knock. However, when prayer is just asking we often grow frustrated when the answers are not immediately forthcoming or not according to our expectations. The experience of Abraham (and to a certain extent, Jonah) shows us that God often uses the process of prayer (*be asking, be seeking, be knocking*) to bring us around to his way of thinking and to understand his mind and perspective on things. In prayer, then, God often changes us to see what he sees and then ask for what he wants.

The Goodness of Affliction

And so, Lord, as I sit here in this dark room, I know you have heard my prayer (as well as the prayers of many others) concerning the outcome of these scans. I have asked you for the things that I want, but you have convinced my heart that this whole situation is not about me and my longevity. It is about you and what you want for my life and the faith of those around me. It is about you being glorified in my body, whether by life or by death. I'm not sure I even understand what that means, but you have brought me to the place where that is what I want. I am in your hands; I bless you, I trust you, and I worship you, my Father. Amen.

31

The Discipline of Affliction

IN DEUTERONOMY 8, MOSES is reviewing the history of God's faithfulness to the new generation of Israel on the cusp of entering the long-awaited Promise Land. The previous generation had died off in the wilderness because of their stubborn refusal to trust God. Numbers 13 records that ten of the twelve men sent into Canaan to spy out the land brought back a negative assessment. They said that while the land flowed with milk and honey, it was also occupied by a people much bigger and stronger, who would devour Israel. This was an affront to the Lord, who had brought them miraculously out of slavery in Egypt, across the Red Sea, defeating Pharaoh's army, and had made them his covenant people during their year-long stay at Sinai. They simply did not trust him and forgot how God had brought them "safe thus far." They even questioned God's motive: "Why is the Lord bringing us into this land, to fall by the sword? Our wives and little ones will become a prey. Would it not be better for us to go back to Egypt?" (Numbers 14:3–4).

Doesn't that sound so much like us—forgetting the blessings of the past because of the issues in the present, casting aspersion on his love for us by questioning his motives for why he has allowed the present circumstances to come upon us? Then we become terrified, because we do not trust him. In Psalm 46 we read, "God is our refuge and strength, a very present help in trouble. Therefore we will not fear, though the earth gives way, though the mountains be moved into the heart of the sea" (verses 1–2). The psalmist tells us that the opposite of fear is not courage, but faith and trust in the God who is our refuge in the face of crisis. So it is at the very point where we are afraid that we are not trusting God.

Thus, Israel failed to trust and God disciplined the nation by closing off the inheritance of the Promised Land to the generation age twenty and above, making them wander in the wilderness for forty years. Moses now addresses this new generation (ages fifty-nine and younger, except for the senior citizens Joshua and Caleb), reminding them of the past and preparing them to enter the land of promise.

Read verses 1–6 and you see that God had humbled the first generation from Egypt to Kadesh Barnea in order to expose their hearts. He humbled them by letting them thirst and get hungry, not to harm them, but so that he could provide for them. Moses specifically mentions how God miraculously provided manna for them and that this physical food was a sign (symbol, metaphor) of something deeper: "man does not live by bread alone, but man lives by every word that comes from the mouth of the Lord." (Deuteronomy 8:3). So it is not the bread that sustains, but the One who provides the bread.

This gives us a perspective on the importance of suffering and affliction in our lives. They reveal what is in our hearts and are designed to bring us to a place where we learn that God is enough. *Suffering is a part of God's discipline (not punishment), to teach us that God alone satisfies.*

Such a perspective has helped me to interpret my own journey with cancer since its diagnosis in April 2017. I was humbled, but my heart was revealed to me. I was brought to a place I had never really been before, a place where I experienced the presence of an All-Sufficient God and his provision for me on a physical level (chemo, surgery). This provision, like manna, was really a sign (a symbol, a metaphor) of something deeper: that I do not live by these medical therapies alone, but by the One who provides them. And now that my cancer has shown itself again, I am prepared to face this new chapter in the journey with the sure and certain hope that he is the All-Sufficient One. He is in control. My life is in the loving hands of my Heavenly Father. Affliction often makes us go deeper in our lives with God and find more than we ever expected.

I was watching an old movie about three prospectors in the California gold rush days who had spent everything on their placer mining claim and equipment and were ready to quit because they had found no gold and were on the edge of starvation. As they were packing up and complaining that it could not get any worse than this, they were suddenly caught in a storm, which blew down a big tree onto their chute and destroyed most of their equipment. That was the final straw!

When the rain finally stopped, they saw that this giant tree was ripped out of the ground and its root system completely exposed. On closer inspection, they saw that entangled in the roots of the tree were pieces of gold and the hole itself left by the roots of the tree was a "glory hole"—a mining term for a depression in the ground that contains a large deposit of gold. They struck it rich in the storm!

Sometimes it takes suffering to help us see the richness of God's glory and provision, and that he is more than enough! "He who has God has everything; he who has everything but God has nothing."[1]

Perhaps affliction has placed you at the border of your own Kadesh Barnea and the Promised Land. You have a choice to make: to cast aspersion on God's character and question his ability to take care of you, or to trust him—that he is enough. This choice must be made every day.

---

1. Attributed to St. Augustine. See https://www.azquotes.com/quote/1290413.

Conclusion

God Has a Greater Interest in Me
Than I Have in Myself

IN CONCLUSION, HERE IS a portion of the book I mentioned in my preface that I would like to share with you. It was written by Thomas Brooks and is titled *A Mute Christian under the Smarting Rod of God: Comfort for Suffering Saints*, originally published in 1659. Here it is:

> "You have a greater interest in me, than I have in myself." The godly one gives himself up to God. The secret language of the soul is this, "Lord, here am I; do with me what you please, I give up myself to be at your disposal."
>
> There was a good woman, who, when she was sick, being asked whether she were willing to live or die, answered, "Whichever God pleases." "But," said one who stood by, "If God would refer it to you, which would you choose?" "Truly," said she, "if God would refer it to me, I would even refer it right back to Him again." This was a soul worth gold.
>
> "Well," says a gracious soul, "the ambitious man gives himself up to his honors, but I give up myself unto God. The voluptuous man gives himself up to his pleasures, but I give up myself to God. The covetous man gives himself up to his bags of money, but I give up myself to God. The wanton man gives himself up to his lust, but I give up myself to God. The drunkard gives himself up to his cups, but I give up myself to God . . . The heretic

gives up himself to his heretical opinions, but I give up myself to God."

Lord! Lay what burden you will upon me, only let your everlasting arms be under me! Strike, Lord, strike, and spare not; for I submit to your will. You have a greater interest in me, than I have in myself; and therefore I give up myself unto you, and am willing to be at your disposal, and am ready to receive whatever impression you shall stamp upon me. O blessed Lord! Have you not again and again said unto me, as once the king of Israel said to the king of Syria, "I am yours, and all that I have is yours" (1 Kings 20:4).

> God says, "I am yours, O soul, to save you!
> My mercy is yours to pardon you!
> My blood is yours to cleanse you!
> My merits are yours to justify you!
> My righteousness is yours to clothe you!
> My Spirit is yours to lead you!
> My grace is yours to enrich you!
> My glory is yours to reward you!"

"And therefore," says a gracious soul, "I cannot but make a resignation of myself unto you. Lord! Here I am, do with me as seems good in your own eyes. I resign up myself to your will."[1]

Amen!

---

1. Brooks, *Mute Christian*, 17.

Bibliography

Bauman, Stephan. *Break Open the Sky*. New York: Crown, 2017.

Blanchard, Charles. *Getting Things from God*. Wheaton, IL: Sword of the Lord, 1953.

Brooks, David. "The Epidemic of Worry." *New York Times*, October 25, 2016. https://www.nytimes.com/2016/10/25/opinion/the-epidemic-of-worry.html.

Brooks, Thomas. *The Mute Christian under the Smarting Rod*. Columbia, SC: First Rate, 2019.

Calvin, John. *Commentary on the Psalms*. Calvin's Commentaries 4. Grand Rapids: Baker, 2003.

Cecil, Richard., ed. *The Works of John Newton*. London: Hamilton, Adams, 1824.

Church of England Evangelical Council. "St. Andrews Day Statement." November 30, 1995. http://www.ceec.info/st-andrews-day-statement.html.

Emanuel, Ezekiel. "Why I Hope to Die at 75." *The Atlantic*, September 2014. http://www.theatlantic.com/features/archive/2014/09/why_i_hope_to_die_at_75/379329/.

The Heidelberg Catechism. Grand Rapids: Faith Alive, 1988.

Hendriksen, William. *More Than Conquerors: An Interpretation of the Book of Revelation*. Grand Rapids: Baker, 1973.

Lewis, C.S. *Mere Christianity*. New York: HarperCollins, 2015.

———. *The Problem of Pain*. New York: Macmillan, 1975

Murray, Ian. *Jonathan Edwards: A New Biography*. Edinburgh: Banner of Truth, 2000.

Niemöller, Martin. "Dachau Sermon Christmas Eve, 1944." In *Christmas Is for the Young: 16 Christmas Sermon Stories*, edited by William Powell Tuch, 55–60. Lima, OH: Children Sermon Service, 2007.

———. "First They Came . . ." Quoted and attributed at https://encyclopedia.ushmm.org/content/en/article/martin-niemoeller-first-they-came-for-the-socialists.

Redman, Matt, and Beth Redman. "Blessed Be Your Name." On *Where Angels Fear to Tread*, 2002. Copyright 2002 Thankyou Music. Lyrics available at

Bibliography

https://www.lyricsfreak.com/m/matt+redman/blessed+be+your+name_20155081.html.

Solzhenitsyn, Aleksandr I. *The Gulag Archipelago, 1918–1956: An Experiment in Literary Investigation*. Vol. 2. New York: Harper & Row, 1976.

Thieliche, Helmut. *The Silence of God*. Translated by G. W. Bromiley. Grand Rapids: Eerdmans, 1966.

Townend, Stuart, and Keith Getty. "In Christ Alone." Copyright © 2001 Thankyou Music. Lyrics available online at https://www.stuarttownend.co.uk/song/in-christ-alone/.

Wiesel, Elie. *Night*. New York: Hill and Wang, 2006.

Made in the USA
Coppell, TX
27 February 2021

50981647R00061